I0225421

# THE MAGNA CARTA OF CARL JUNG

The Ananlytical Typology Co.

We dedicate this work to the memory of Carl Gustav Jung in gratitude for the rich legacy he imparted to humanity for a more comprehensive understanding of the human psyche.

# THE MAGNA CARTA
# OF
# CARL JUNG

## A Critical Psychology

Extracted and compiled by Frederik Huysamen,
Linda Stroebel and Elmarie Malek

Copyright © The Magna Carta of Carl Jung
by Frederik Huysamen, Linda Stroebel and Elmarie Malek. All rights reserved.
Published by The Analytical Typology Co.
Cell +27 (0)82 462 0858
liaison@analytical-typology.com
analytical-typology.com

Cover artwork and page layout design by Sumi Creative Co.
First edition, first print, 2023
Revised edition, 2024
ISBN 978-0-7961-7232-7

"Above all you must realise that I am not in the habit of interfering with my pupils. I have neither the right nor the might to do that. They can draw such conclusions as seem right to them and must accept full responsibility for it. There have been so many pupils of mine who have fabricated every sort of rubbish from what they took over from me."

– C.G. *Jung Letters vol. 1*, p. 518

# CONTENTS

# EDITORIAL NOTE

The original 1923 English translation of C.G. Jung's *Psychological Types* by H.G. Baynes was republished in 1971 as Volume 6 of the English 20-volume *The Collected Works of C.G. Jung,* as a revision by R.F.C. Hull. In the process, many of the finer nuances of Jung's original material in the German version were distorted. Similar variances have been noted in the Hull revision of the English translations of the first three* of the *Four Papers on Psychological Typology* in the *Appendix* of *Psychological Types* [*consecutively translated by Constance E. Long (1913/1916); H.G. Baynes and Cary F. Baynes (1925/1928); W.S. Dell and Cary F. Baynes (1931/1933)].

Towards ensuring a dynamic equivalent presentation of Jung's original conceptualisation, *The Magna Carta of Carl Jung* makes use of (i) the English translations of *Psychological Types* (1923 & 1971) and the three related papers mentioned above; and (ii) our own translation of a few references from the original German texts of *Psychologische Typen* (1921, p. 5 & p. 701) and the fourth paper (1936, p. 264, p. 266, p. 267, p. 271 & p. 272), as well as the Hull translation, referenced correspondingly throughout as "§".

Annotations have been included in square brackets in instances where references require contextualisation. Repetition of some references for the purpose of optimising the flow of content has been necessary. American spelling has been exchanged for English spelling.

# FOREWORD

The year of 2023 marked the centenary of the publication of the English translation of Carl Jung's eminent work, *Psychological Types*, first published in German in 1921. The original 1923 English translation was the work of Jung's assistant in Zurich at that time, H.G. (also known as Peter) Baynes. Of importance is that it is the only translation of any of Jung's books into any language that Jung himself went through word for word [Hannah, B. (1997) *Jung: His Life and Work*. p.140].

*The Magna Carta of Carl Jung* represents Jung's view of psychological types as **a critical psychology**: It represents the fundamental principles of and criteria for the psychological types in a format that can serve as a critical tool when applying Jung's theory in practice.

*The Magna Carta of Carl Jung* represents Jung's critical concepts of his psychological type theory in his own words. This is the first direct representation of his critical concepts for the educated layperson: the linguist, neuroscientist, artificial intelligence investigator, social psychologist, psychotherapist, mediator, academic, educator, author, scholar – in short, any individual who is genuinely interested in a more in-depth understanding of the human psyche and the development of personality. Seen in perspective, the development of artificial intelligence is limited by the measure of grasp and objective understanding of Carl Jung's analytical psychology, starting with the psychological processes of decisiveness, which in current speech is referred to as decision-making. There is much more to the human psyche than what we think we know about ourselves.

*The Magna Carta of Carl Jung* presents, succinctly and incrementally, a complete series of stepping-stones that offer the reader a grasp of the unfolding of Jung's gradual concept-building towards his whole psychological typology: the distilling of his conceptual process that took place over the course of twenty years. Direct reference is made throughout to Jung's original conceptualisations of typological complexities, which reflect his brilliant thinking.

*The Magna Carta of Carl Jung* is not a summary, but rather a footpath alongside the developing stream of Jung's conceptualisation process towards defining his psychological typology. It thus provides a solid footing to enable a stepwise understanding of Jung's far-reaching insights. It is presented in narrative format, understandable by the audience for whom Jung intended it: educated lay persons of all psychological typologies. As he states in his foreword: "The psychological points of view presented in this book are of wide significance and application." So too in his conclusion: "The fact of the different typological attitudes is a problem of the first order, not only for psychology but also for all those departments of science and life in which human psychology plays a decisive role." [1923, p. 7 & p. 619].

– Frederik Huysamen, Linda Stroebel, Elmarie Malek
Cape Town 2024

# INTRODUCTION

The psychological typology of Carl Jung forms a definite and profoundly important aspect of human psychology. It is marked by the concept of "decisiveness", which in modern speech is referred to as decision-making. *Psychological Types* is therefore a typology of the different modes of decisiveness. It is the first and only *purely psychological* typology ever developed.

*The Magna Carta of Carl Jung* is a meticulously considered extraction and compilation of Jung's concepts, presented in his own words, from his book, *Psychological Types*. It thus provides a direct representation of Jung's core concepts about psychological types.

This book frames these core concepts in a unique sequence which allows the reader to follow the unfolding of Jung's discoveries in a step-by-step manner. This approach traverses the historical and empirical grounds that give rise to the developmental trajectory of Jung's concepts, affording readers the opportunity to obtain a grasp of Jung's comprehensive discoveries about psychological types for themselves.

The book distils Jung's essential concepts into an authentic rendition thereof, making it accessible to the audience for which Jung intended it: the educated layman. Its value for all individuals on their journey of self-discovery is perhaps best described in Jung's own words: "I would not for anything dispense with this compass on my psychological voyages of discovery." [*Collected Works* Vol. 6, §959]

Carl Jung formulates the following typological requirement as a key principle in *Psychological Types* by saying that "every theory of the psychic processes must submit to be valued in its turn … as the expression of an existing and recognized type of human psychology." (1923, p. 628) Herewith Jung expresses the direct relation between a specific psychological theory and the typological composition of its author. The said key principle binds us to view Jung's theory of psychological types as an expression of his function type. Non-compliance of this key principle serves as a single point of failure.

In his Foreword to the 1921 Swiss edition, Jung describes for example the decision making capacity by which he arrived at his typological conceptualization, as follows: "Es ist gedanklich allmählich entstanden," translated as "It is a gradua intellectual structure." (1921, p. 5; 1923, p. 7) Jung states unequivocally: "Intellectual" or "intellect" refers to the individual's "faculty of directed thinking." (1923, p. 611) He equates the psychological meaning of the term "intellectual" with conscious or directed "thinking." Jung is consistent in his use of the term "intellectual." It refers exclusively to the thinking function. Jung, without doubt, classifies himself as the intellectual type.

*The Magna Carta of Carl Jung* is divided into four sections, comprising 456 references. It is imperative that the sections and the individual references be read in order of sequence. The sections consist of a number of sub-headings, each of which presents a particular theme touched on by Jung in *Psychological Types*.

Section I provides important perspectives – historical and contextual – which frame Jung's process of concept-building of psychological types.

Section II collates the precision concepts, principles and criteria which Jung developed for an exact scientific understanding of his discoveries about the four basic psychological function-types.

Section III presents Jung's discoveries regarding the flow and direction of psychic energy in relation to the four functions – the two attitude types of introversion and extraversion – and their modifying effect on the four function-types.

Section IV expands on certain aspects and contextualises the functions of consciousness in relation to the unconscious.

The paragraph sign and number at the end of quotations, for example "§987", correlates with the paragraph numbering of the popular 1971 English translation of *Collected Works* Vol. 6.

**Bold font** is used to emphasise key words or phrases and facilitate conceptual links.

# SECTION I

## PSYCHOLOGICAL TYPES: HISTORICAL AND CONTEXTUAL PERSPECTIVES

# Mind and body

**01** (1933, p. 85)
The **distinction** between **mind and body** is **an artificial dichotomy**, a discrimination which is unquestionably based far more on the peculiarity of **intellectual understanding** than on the **nature** of things. §916

**02** (1933, p. 85)
The **continuity** of **nature** knows nothing of those antithetical distinctions which the **human intellect** is forced to set up as **aids to understanding**. §915

**03** (1971)
Somewhere the psyche is **living body**, and the living body is **animated matter**; somehow and somewhere there is an undiscoverable **unity** of **psyche and body** which would need **investigating psychically** as well as **physically**; in other words, this **unity** must be as **dependent** on the **body** as it is on the **psyche** so far as the investigator is concerned. §961

**04** (1933, p. 85)
So intimate is the intermingling of bodily and psychic traits that not only can we **draw** far-reaching **inferences** as to the constitution of the psyche **from the constitution of the body**, but we can also **infer from psychic peculiarities** the corresponding bodily characteristics. The latter process is more difficult. In taking **the mind as our starting-point** we work our way from the **relatively unknown** to the known; while in the opposite case we have the advantage of **starting** from something **known**, that is, from **the visible body**. §916

**05** (1933, p. 86-87)
Merely to establish the fact that certain people have this or that appearance is of **no significance if it does not allow us to infer a psychic correlative**. We have learned something only when we have determined what mental attributes go with a given bodily constitution. §918

**06** (1933, p. 87)
The **body** means little to us **without** the **psyche**. §918

# Science and materialism

**07** (1971)
The particular **mental product** that far **surpassed** all the achievements of the ancient world was **science**. §965

**08** (1971)
The **materialism** of the **nineteenth century** gave the **body first place** and **relegated** the **psyche** to the rank of something secondary and derived, allowing it no more substantiality than that of a so-called "**epiphenomenon.**" §961

**09** (German, 1936, p. 264)
The **assumption** that *physical processses* determine *psychic phenomena* was in itself a good **working hypothesis** that became, with the emergence of materialism, a philosophical assertion. §961

**10** (1971)
Any **serious science** of the living organism will reject **this presumption**; for on the one hand it will constantly bear in mind that **living matter** is **an as yet unsolved mystery**, and on the other hand it will be objective enough to recognise that for us there is a completely unbridgeable **gulf** between **physical** and **psychic phenomena**, so that **the psychic realm** is **no less mysterious** than **the physical**. §961

**11** (1971)
**Science** brought about a splendid **rehabilitation** of **matter**, and in this respect materialism may even be regarded as an act of historical justice. §965

## Scientific investigation of the psyche

**12** (German, 1936, p. 266)
The human psyche, which is an absolutely essential area of experience, remained for a very long time a metaphysical reserve, although there have been **increasingly** serious **attempts to open up** the essence of **the psyche** to **scientific observation** since the Enlightenment. §966

**13** (1971)
They **began**, tentatively, with the **sense perceptions**, and gradually ventured into the **domain of associations**. This line of research paved the way for **experimental psychology**, and it culminated in the "**physiological psychology**" of Wundt. §966

**14** (1933, p. 86)
There are **any number of paths** leading *from without*, inward, *from the physical* to the **psychic**. §917

**15** (1933, p. 86)

It appears **safer for us** to **proceed** from the outer world inward, from the known to the unknown, **from the body to the mind**. §917

**16** (1933, p. 86)

It is **necessary** that research should **follow** this direction **until** certain **elementary psychic facts** are established with sufficient certainty. The **first requirement** is to **establish** the **primary facts of psychic life**. §917

**17** (1933, p. 86)

We have only just **begun** the work of **compiling** an **inventory of the psyche**, and our results have not always been successful. §917

**18** (1933, p. 86)

**Unfortunately** we are **not yet** far **enough advanced** to **answer** this question even **roughly**. §917

**19** (1933, p. 86)

Once having established **these facts**, we can **reverse the procedure**. We can then put the question: What are the **bodily correlatives** of a given **psychic condition**? §917

**20** (1933, p. 87)

The **psyche** means little to us **without** the **body**. §918

## Holistic approach to the psyche

**21** (1971)

A **descriptive** kind of **psychology** developed in **France**. Its chief exponents were **Taine**, **Ribot**, and **Janet**. It was characteristic of this **scientific approach** that it **broke down the psyche** into particular **mechanisms or processes**. §966

**22** (German, 1936, p. 266)

**Beyond these attempts**, some individuals **aspired** to what we today would describe as **a holistic view** [the unity of the psyche]. §966

**23** (German, 1936, p. 266)

The **names** of William James, Freud and Flournoy are *linked* **to this line** of contemporary scientific **endeavours**. James and his Swiss friend, Théodore Flournoy, attempted to **describe psychic phenomena** in its entirety and to **judge** the **psyche** as a **unity**. §967

**24** (1971)
**Freud, too**, as a doctor, took as **his point of departure** the **wholeness** and **indivisibility** of the **human personality**, though, in keeping with the **spirit of the age**, he **restricted himself** to the **investigation** of **instinctive mechanisms** and **individual processes**. §967

**25** (German, 1936, p. 267)
He also **narrowed** the entirety of the human [psyche] to the picture of an essentially "bourgeois" [civil] *collective person*, which gave rise to a **one-sided** ideological interpretation. §967

**26** (German, 1936, p. 267)
Unfortunately Freud **succumbed** to the medical man's **temptation to trace back every psychic phenomenon to the body**. §967

**27** (1971)
Freud, after a proper psychological start, **reverted** to the **ancient assumption** of the **sovereignty** of the **physical constitution**, trying to **turn everything back** in theory into **instinctual** processes **conditioned** by the **body**. §968

**28** (1923, p. 565)
When I speak of **instinct**, I therewith denote an *impulsion* towards certain activities. **Every psychic phenomenon** is **instinctive** which *proceeds* **from dynamic impulsion** and **not from a cause postulated by the will**. §765


## The sovereignty of the psyche

**29** (German, 1936, p. 267)
**I start** from the **assumption** of the **independence** of the **psyche**. §968

**30** (1971)
Since body and psyche somewhere form a unity, although in their manifest natures they are so utterly different, **we cannot but attribute** to the **one** as to **the other** a **substantiality** of **its own**. §968

**31** (German, 1936, p. 267)
As long as we do not know this unity in any way, we have **no option** but to **inves-**

tigate body and soul [psyche] **separately** and in the first instance **treat them** as if they were **independent of each other**, at least in their structure. §968

**32** (1971)
That they are not so, we can see for ourselves every day. But **if we stop** at that, we would **never** be in a position to make out **anything about the psyche** at all. §968

**33** (German, 1936, p. 267)
If we now assume the **independence of the soul** [psyche], then we **free ourselves** – for the time being – from the **unsolvable task** of **tracing everything psychic** back to a **specific physical thing**. §96

**34** (German, 1936, p. 267)
We can then **take the manifestations of the psyche** as **expressions of its own nature** and attempt to **establish laws** or **types**. §969

## The uniformity and diversity of the psyche

**35** (1923, p. 622)
**Every theory** of complex psychic processes **presupposes** a uniform *human psychology*. §849

**36** (1923, p. 624)
If I establish a **theory** upon that which **connects all** [what is common to all], I explain the psyche from that which is its **foundation** and **origin**. §852

**37** (1923, p. 624-5)
**In so doing**, my **explanation** entirely **omits** that **factor** which **consists in its** [human as subject] historical or **individual differentiation**. With such a theory, I **ignore** the **psychology of the conscious psyche**. Therewith I actually deny **the whole other side of the psyche**, namely, **its differentiation from** the **primordial germinal state**. §852

**38** (1923, p. 627)
In the case of **a psychological theory** the necessity of a **plurality of explanations** is **definitely granted**, since, unlike any other natural science theory [scientific theory], the **object** of psychological explanation **is of like nature** with the **subject:** *one psychological process has to explain another* [in contrast to a Nature-process which is largely independent of human psychology]. §855

**39** (1971)
If one is plunged into the chaos of psychological opinions, prejudices, and susceptibilities, one gets a **profound** and **indelible impression** of the **diversity** of individual **psychic dispositions**, **tendencies**, and **convictions**. (Foreword to the Argentine Edition, p. xiv)

**40** (1923, p. 624)
The **notion** of a **uniformity** of the *conscious* psyche is an **academic chimera**. §851

**41** (1923, p. 620)
**Strife** and **misunderstanding** are constant requisites for the **tragi-comedy of human life**. §847

**42** (1923, p. 620)
**In smaller things** a prevailing superficiality may help to build a **bridge** over the chasm which lack of understanding makes between man and man. But, **in more important matters** and especially those wherein the ideal of the type is in question, an **understanding** seems, as a rule, to be **beyond** the **limits of possibility**. §847

**43** (1923, p. 620)
It is a **fact**, which is constantly and overwhelmingly apparent in one's practical work, that a man is well-nigh **incapable** [virtually incapable] of **comprehending** and giving **full sanction** to *any other standpoint than his own*. §847

## Transfer disputes to the psychological realm

**44** (1923, p. 619-20)
**Every philosophy** that is not just a mere history of philosophy **depends** upon a **personal psychological precondition** [premise]. What we regarded as **individual prejudice** is certainly **not so** under all circumstances; since the **standpoint of the philosopher in question** often **boasts** a very **imposing following**. His standpoint is **acceptable** to these men not because they echo him without thinking, but **because** it is something **they** can **fully understand** and appreciate. Such an understanding would be quite impossible if the standpoint of the philosopher were merely individually determined, for it is quite certain in that case that he would neither be fully understood nor even tolerated. The **peculiar character of the standpoint** which is understood and appreciated by his following must, therefore,

correspond with a typical personal attitude, which in the same or similar form finds **many representatives** in human society. §846

**45** (1923, p. 620)
As a rule, the **partisans** of either side **attack each other** *merely externally*, always **seeking out** the **joints** [vulnerable spots] in their **opponent's individual armour**. *Such* a dispute, as a rule, bears **little fruit**. §846

**46** (1923, p. 620)
It would be of considerably greater value if the **contest** were **transferred** to the **psychological realm**, whence it actually originates. §846

## The need for order among the many points of view

**47** (1971)
One feels the **need** for some kind of **order** among the chaotic multiplicity of points of view. (Foreword to the Argentine Edition, p. xiv)

**48** (1971)
The research worker needs definite points of view and guidelines if he is to **reduce** the **chaotic profusion** of **individual experiences** to any **kind of order**. §986

**49** (1971)
This need calls for a **critical orientation** and for **general principles** and **criteria**, not too specific in their formulation, which may serve as ***points de repère*** in sorting out the **empirical material**. (Foreword to the Argentine Edition, p. xiv)

**50** (1923, p. 620)
Such a **transposition** [to the psychological realm] would soon reveal the fact that **many different kinds** of **psychological attitudes** [different modes of decision-making] exist, **each** of which has a **right to existence**, although necessarily leading to the setting up of incompatible theories. §846

**51** (1923, p. 621)
It is my conviction that **a basis for the adjustment of conflicting views** could be found in the **recognition of different types of attitude**, not however of the mere **existence** of such types but also of **the fact that every man** is so **imprisoned** in **his type** that he is simply **incapable** of a **complete understanding of another standpoint**. Without a **recognition** of this far-reaching demand a **violation** of the

other's standpoint is practically **inevitable**. §847

**52** (1923, p. 11)
This recognition of types of attitude may prove a **clarifying contribution** to a **dilemma** which, not in **analytical psychology** alone but also in **other provinces of science**, and especially in the personal relations of human beings one to another, has led and still continues to lead to **misunderstanding** and **division** [discord]. §4

**53** (1923, p. 619)
The **fact** of the **different typical attitudes** is a **problem** of the **first order**, not only for **psychology** but also for all those departments of **science** and life in which **human psychology** plays a **decisive** role. §846

# Earliest attempts to classify individuals according to types

**54** (1933, p. 94)
Since the earliest times, **attempts** have repeatedly been made to **classify individuals** according to **types**, and thus **to bring order** into the confusion [of opinions]. §933

**55** (1928, p. 295)
Since ancient times there have been attempts to break down the **apparent uniformity** of mankind by a **sharper characterisation** of certain *typical differences*. §883

**56** (1933, p. 86)
In ancient times, **astrology** even turned to **stellar space** in order to determine those lines of fate whose beginnings are contained in man himself. To the same class of interpretations **from outward** signs belong palmistry, Gall's phrenology, Lavater's study of physiognomy, and more recently, graphology, Kreschmer's physiological types, and Rorschach's klexographic method. §917

**57** (1933, p. 86)
**All attempts** at **characterology** have started **from the outside** world. §917

**58** (1933, p. 95)
Our scientific conscience no longer permits us to revert to **these old**, intuitive **ways** of **handling the question**. §934

# Psychological types and science

**59** (1933, p. 95)
We must find our own **answer** to this problem, an answer which **satisfies** the **demands of science**. §934

**60** (1923, p. 623)
I am quite convinced that a **Nature-process** which is **largely independent** of human psychology, and **therefore can only be an object** for it [the human as subject], can have but **one true explanation**. §850

**61** (1923, p. 75)
**Science**, under all circumstances, is **an affair** of the **intellect**, and the other psychological functions are submitted to it in the form of objects. The **intellect** is the **sovereign** of the **scientific realm**. §84

**62** (1923, p. 611)
**Intellectual** or **intellect** refers to the individual's **faculty** of directed **thinking**. §832

**63** (1923, p. 611)
The term **"thinking"** should be **confined** to the **linking up of representations** by means of a **concept**. §831

**64** (1923, p. 611)
To my mind, a simple **stringing together** of **representations** [thus lacking conceptions] is **not thinking at all**, but mere *presentation*. §831

**65** (1923, p. 611)
The faculty of directed thinking, I term intellect. Thinking **arranges** the **representations *under concepts* in accordance** with the **presuppositions** of my conscious **rational norm**. §832

**66** (1923, p. 570)
**Only** an **object** that has been **postulated** can also be **completely explained** on rational grounds, since it has **never** contained **anything beyond what was postulated** by rational thinking. §775

**67** (1923, p. 16)
The ideal and the **purpose** of **science** do **not** consist in giving the most exact possible **description of the facts** – science cannot yet compete with cinematographic

and phonographic records – it can fulfil its aim and purpose only in the **establishment of law**, which is merely an abbreviated **expression** for **manifold** and yet **correlated processes**. This purpose **transcends** the **purely experimental** by means of the *concept*, which has general and proved validity. §9

**68** (1923, p. 518)
There is the **difficulty** that the **material of experience** [psychological], the **object of scientific consideration, cannot be displayed in concrete form** [presented directly], as it were, to the eyes of the reader. §672

**69** (1933, p. 89)
**We ourselves are psyches** [the object of scientific investigation]. §920

**70** (1933, p. 96)
**Whatever** we look at, and **however** we look at it, we see **only** through our **own eyes.** §936

**71** (1923, p. 16)
The **operation** of the **personal equation has already begun** in the act of **observation.** §9

**72** (1923, p. 16)
There is a **psychological personal equation**, *not* merely a *psychophysical*. We can see colours [psychological], but not *wave-lengths* [quantitatively measurable]. §9

**73** (1923, p. 518)
Only in so far as **elementary facts** are **accessible to number and measure** can there be any question of a **direct presentation**. §672

**74** (1923, p. 518)
My **association studies** have demonstrated that highly complicated psychological phenomena are accessible to **methods of measure**. §672

**75** (1923, p. 518)
But **how much** of the actual psychology of man can be **witnessed** and **observed** as **measurable facts?** §672

**76** (1933, p. 89; German, 1921, p. 571)
The **more** we turn from **spatial phenomena** and come to deal with the **spaceless psyche**, the **more impossible** it becomes to determine anything by **exact measurement**. §921

**77** (1923, p. 518-19)
Anyone who has probed more deeply into the nature of psychology, demanding something more of it than science in the wretchedly prescribed limits of a natural science method [quantitative measurement] is able to yield, will also have realised that **an experimental method** [quantitative measurement] **will never succeed** in doing justice to the nature of the human soul, **nor will it ever trace** even an approximately **faithful picture of the complicated psychic phenomena**. §672

**78** (1923, p. 518)
The **psychological investigator** is always finding himself obliged to make **use of extensive description** for the presentation of the reality he has observed. §672

**79** (1923, p. 519)
In order to escape the **drawback** this **overvaluation** of the natural science method [quantitative measurement] involves, **one is obliged to have recourse to well-defined** *concepts*. §674

**80** (1923, p. 519)
When we leave the **realm of measurable facts**, we are dependent upon *concepts*, which have now to **assume the office** [function] **of measure and number**. §673

**81** (1923, p. 519)
That **precision** which **exact measurements** lend to the **observed fact** can be **replaced** only by the ***precision of the concept***. §673

**82** (1923, p. 518)
**In psychological work especially**, one cannot proceed too **cautiously** when dealing with **concepts** and **expressions** [terminology]. §672

**83** (1923, p. 519-20)
The **individual pioneer** must at least strive to give **his concepts** some **fixity** and **precision**; and this is best achieved by so elucidating the **meaning** of the **concepts** he employs as to put everyone in a position to see what he **means** by them. §674

**84** (1971)
The **typological system** I have proposed is an attempt to provide an **explanatory** basis [thinking system] and theoretical framework for the **boundless diversity** that has hitherto prevailed in the **formation** of **psychological concepts**. §987

**85** (1923, p. 546)
The **very idea** [rationale] of a **classification** is **intellectual** [directed thinking]. §728

# Jung's point of reference

**86** (1933, p. 96)
I do not know how other people would set about the **task**. I can therefore only tell you how **I myself have approached the matter**, and I must submit to the reproach that **my way** of **solving the problem** is the outcome of **my individual prejudice** [directed thinking]. §936

**87** (1971)
My concern is to show how the **ideas** I have **abstracted** can be **linked up** historically and terminologically with an existing body of knowledge. I have done this from a desire to bring the **experiences** of a **medical specialist** [psychiatrist] out of their narrow professional setting into a **more general context** which will **enable** the **educated layman** to derive some **profit** from them. (Foreword to the First Swiss Edition, p. xi)

**88** (1933, p. 101-2)
In **social life** a **rough grouping of this sort** [of merely individual events] has long ago come about, and as a result we have types like the *peasant*, the *worker*, the *artist*, the *scholar*, the *warrior*, and so forth down the list of the various professions. But **this sort** of **typification** has very little **to do with psychology**. §948

**89** (1933, p. 102)
A **type theory** must be **subtle** [differentiated]. §949

**90** (1933, p. 102)
It is not enough, **for example**, to speak of **intelligence**, for this is **too general** and **too vague** a concept. **Intelligence**, like stupidity, is *not* a *function* but a **modality**; the term tells us nothing more than *how* a function works. §949

**91** (1928, p. 295-96)
**Galen** deserves the credit of having created a **psychological classification** of **human individuals** [the first attempt at a typology] which has endured for two thousand years, a classification which rests upon **perceptible** differences of *emotional* or *affective* [temperaments] constitution. §884

**92** (1928, p. 296)
It is **interesting** to note that the **first attempt at classification of types** is **concerned** with the **emotional behaviour** of men; manifestly because the play of emotion forms the **most** frequent and obviously **striking feature** of any **behaviour**. §884

**93** (1923, p. 522)
I use **emotion** as **synonymous** with **affect**. §681

**94** (1928, p. 296)
**Affects** are revealed at once, even to superficial observation. §885

**95** (1928, p. 300)
It is impossible to deny that the **condition** of **affect pertains to the ego.** §891

**96** (1928, p. 300)
In the **affective state** the ego is **unfree, driven, in a state of compulsion.** §891

**97** (1928, p. 300)
The **affective state** has the **character** of either a **falsification** of the "real" personality, or **as not belonging** to ego-consciousness as an authentic attribute. §891

**98** (1923, p. 351)
In the **deepest affects** [emotions], the *distinctions* of type are **at once obliterated.** §474

**99** (1928, p. 299)
If **affect** is used as the criterion, the **general agreement** which **science demands** can **never be reached.** §889

**100** (1928, p. 299)
In **complete contrast to** the **old system of classification** according to **temperaments** [affects], the problem of a **new typology begins** with the **convention,** *neither* to **allow** oneself to be **judged by affect,** *nor* so to **judge others by affect,** since, as a final statement, no one will admit himself to be identical with his affect. §889

**101** (1928, p. 300)
**In contrast to** the **affective state,** the **normal state** [ego-consciousness] is understood as a **condition of free-choice,** of disposability of one's mental powers. §891

**102** (1923, p. 351)
**In my construction** of concepts, I am **starting** out from the fact of **differentiated psyches.** §853

**103** (1928, p. 300)
We must take as our **criterion** that **condition** or **attitude** which is felt by the ob-

ject [the individual] to be a **conscious, normal state of mind**. §891

**104** (1923, p. 453)
I **base** my **judgement** upon what the individual feels to be his **conscious psychology**. §601

**105** (1923, p. 535)
By **consciousness** I understand the **relatedness** of **psychic contents to the ego**, in so far as **they are sensed as such by the ego**. §700

**106** (1923, p. 536)
There exist a **great many** psychic complexes and these are **not all**, **necessarily**, **connected** with the **ego**. §700

**107** (1923, p. 535)
In so far as **relations** are **not sensed as such** by the ego, they are **unconscious**. §700

**108** (1923, p. 453)
[I base] my presentation on the subjective **conscious psychology** of the individual [ego-consciousness versus inferior unconscious psychology], since there, at least, one has a **definite objective footing**. §601

## The psychomotor apparatus [execution] versus the psychic apparatus [decisiveness]

**109** (1933, p. 93)
The question is: **How** does a person **react** to an **obstacle**? §930

**110** (1933, p. 93)
For instance, we come to a **brook** where there is **no bridge**. The stream is **too broad** to step across, and we **must jump**. §930

**111** (1933, p. 93)
**To make this possible**, we have at our disposal a complicated functional system, namely, the **psycho-motor system**. It is completely developed and needs only to be released. §930

**112** (1933, p. 93)
But **before this** happens, **something** of a **purely psychic nature** takes place, that

is, the **decision** is made about what is to be done. §930

**113** (1933, p. 93)
Just as the psycho-motor apparatus is automatically at our disposal, so there is an **exclusively psychic apparatus** ready for our use in the **making of decisions**. §930

**114** (1923, p. 619)
We are here **concerned** only with the **psychological problem** [psychic apparatus]. §846

**115** (1923, p. 206)
I **altogether exclude** the **factor of activity** [behaviour] as a point of view. §273

# Investigate the individual's empirical material

**116** (1923, p. 15-16)
There are indeed not a few who hold that a psychology can be written ***ex cathedra***. Nowadays, however, most of us are **convinced** that **an objective psychology** must above all, be **grounded** upon **observation and experience**. §9

**117** (1928, p. 307)
The **scientific investigator** cannot content itself with an intuition, but must **concern** itself with the **actual material presented**. §903

# The psychic apparatus for decision-making

**118** (1933, p. 102)
We must be able to **designate** what it is that **functions outstandingly** [psychic apparatus] in the individual's habitual way of reacting. §949

**119** (1933, p. 93)
Opinions **differ widely** as to **what** this **apparatus is like**. §931

**120** (1971)
It is **certain only** that every individual has his **accustomed way** of **making decisions** [*a priori* to execution] and dealing with difficulties. §931

**121** (1933, p. 94)
But just as **crystals** show **basic uniformities** which are relatively simple, so do

these **personal attitudes** [the different accustomed ways of making decisions] show certain **fundamental traits** which allow us to **assign** them to **definite groups**. §932

**122** (1933, p. 100)
To **observe** and **recognise** the **differences** gave me comparatively little trouble. §945

**123** (1933, p. 100)
The root of my difficulties being now **the problem** of **criteria**. §945

**124** (1933, p. 95)
Here we meet the **chief difficulty** of the problem of types – that is, **the question of standards or criteria**. §934

**125** (1933, p. 100)
How was I to find **the right terms** for the characteristic differences? §945

**126** (1933, p. 100)
I have realised that **no sound criteria** are to be found **in the chaos of contemporary psychology**. §946

**127** (1933, p. 100)
They have first to be **made** [created]. §946

**128** (1933, p. 102)
However difficult it is to define such notions *scientifically* and thus make of them **psychological concepts**, they are easily **intelligible** in **current speech**. §949

**129** (1933, p. 103)
Everyone knows, **for example**, what **consciousness** is, and nobody doubts that the concept covers a **definite psychic condition**, however **far** science may be **from defining** it **satisfactorily**. §949

**130** (1933, p. 102)
**Speech** is a **storehouse** of **images** founded on experience, and therefore **concepts** which are **too abstract** do not easily take root in it, or quickly die out again for **lack of contact with reality**. §949

# SECTION II

## THE FOUR FUNCTION-TYPES: CONCEPTS, PRINCIPLES AND CRITERIA

# The four basic functions of orientation

**131** (1923, p. 14)
As **basic functions**, that is, functions which are both **genuinely** as well as **essentially differentiated from other functions** [will-power, temperament, imagination, memory, morality, etc.], there exist *thinking*, *feeling*, *sensation*, and *intuition*. §7

**132** (1933, p. 103)
I simply formed my **concepts** of the psychic functions from the notions expressed in **current speech**, and used them as my **criteria** in **judging** the differences [in the accustomed ways individuals make decisions]. §950

**133** (1933, p. 103)
**For example**, I took **thinking** as it is generally understood, because I was struck by the fact that many persons habitually [predominantly] do more thinking than others, and accordingly give more weight to thoughts when making important decisions [intellectual conclusions]. They also use their thinking in trying to **understand** and adapt themselves to the world, and whatever happens to them is subjected to consideration and reflection, or at least **reconciled** with some **principle** [norm] **sanctioned by thought**. §950

**134** (1923, p. 570)
Empirical science **postulates rationally limited objects** [which are confined within rational bounds]. §775

# Definitions of the four function-types

**135** (1971)
When the numinal accent [the predominant, determining, and decisive quality] falls on *thinking*, judgement [intellectual conclusion] is reserved as to what **significance** [norm or law or full conceptual understanding of a formulated problem] should be attached to the *facts in question* [only for that area of the object which is being considered]. And on this significance will depend the way in which the individual deals with the facts [in question]. §984

**136** (German, 1936, p. 271)
If the *feeling* is numinal, the adjustment depends entirely on what **emotional value** is attributed to a fact. §984 & §903

**137** (German, 1936, p. 271)

There are ... people for whom the numinal accent falls on *sensation*, i.e. the perception of **actualities**, and raises these to the exclusive condition and the direction-giving principle. These are the fact-minded people, for whom intellectual judgment, feeling and intuition are in the background in relation to the overriding significance of the actual facts. [The basic psychological function of sensation should not be confused with the physiological sense organs] §984.

**138** (1971)

Finally, if the numinal accent falls on *intuition*, actual reality counts only in so far as it seems to harbour possibilities which then become the supreme motivating force, regardless of the way things actually are in the present. §984

**139** (1923, p. 14)

In order to ensure the **clarity** which is **essential** in such complicated things, I have devoted the **last chapter** of this book [*Psychological Types,* chapter XI] to **the definitions** of **my** psychological **conceptions**. §7

# Relative contribution of each one of the four function-types

**140** (1971)

The **localisation** of the **numinal accent** thus gives rise to **four function-types**. §985

**141** (1923, p. 547)

I **differentiate** these functions **from one another**, because they are *neither* mutually **relatable** *nor* mutually **reducible**. §731

**142** (1923, p. 127)

**Only one part of the world** can be *comprehended* through *thinking*, **another part only** through *feeling*, **a third only through** *sensation*, [and **another part only** by intuition]. §158

**143** (1928, p. 307)

Let us take **for example** an **intellectual** [thinking] type; most of **the conscious material** which he **presents to observation** is directly dependent on intellectual **premises**. §903

**144** (1923, p. 127)

**Thinking**, under all circumstances **commands** [claims] **only a third or a fourth** of the **total significance**, although **in its own sphere** it possesses **exclusive validity**. §158

**145** (1928, p. 305)

For a **complete** orientation of consciousness, **all four** functions **should cooperate equally.** §900

## Limitations of the four psychological functions in the individual

**146** (1923, p. 28)

**Every man**, as a relatively stable being, possesses **all the basic psychological functions.** §28

**147** (1923, p. 563-4)

Experience shows that it is **hardly possible** for anyone to bring **all** his psychological functions to **simultaneous** development. §763

**148** (1923, p. 434)

The four basic psychological functions **seldom or never** have the **same strength** or **grade of development** in one and the same individual. §584

**149** (1928, p. 306)

**In reality** it is **seldom or never** that these four fundamental functions are uniformly developed and **correspondingly disposable by the will.** §901

**150** (1928, p. 306)

As a rule **one or another** function is in the **foreground** [in differentiated individuals], while the **rest** remain in the **background** [in the unconscious], relatively or quite **undifferentiated.** §901

**151** (1923, p. 434)

As a rule, **one or the other** function **predominates**, in both **strength** and **development.** §584

**152** (1928, p. 308)

As a rule **only one** [of the four basic functions] is **fully conscious** and **differentiated**, so that it is **free** and **subject** to the **direction of the will.** §905

**153** (1923, p. 514)
We speak of the **consciousness** of a **function** only when not merely **its application** is **at the disposal of the will**, but when **at the same time its principle** is **decisive** for the **orientation of consciousness**. §667

**154** (1923, p. 514)
This is true when, **for instance,** *thinking* is not a mere afterthought, or rumination, but when its decisions possess an **absolute validity**, so that the logical **conclusion** in a given case holds good, *whether* as motive *or* as a **guarantee of practical action**, without the backing of any further evidence. §667

**155** (1923, p. 514)
This **absolute sovereignty** always belongs, empirically, to **one function alone**. §667

**156** (1923, p. 535)
**Consciousness** is the **relatedness** of psychic contents **to the ego**. §700

**157** (1923, p. 613)
**The unconscious** covers **all those psychic contents or processes** which are not conscious, that is, *not related to the ego in a perceptible way*. §837

## Variant terminologies for the principal function regardless of whether it is thinking, feeling, sensation or intuition

**158**
**Principal** function … (1971, p. 405 & 1923, p. 513)
**Primary** function … §667 (1923, p. 514)
**Dominant** function … §667 (1971)
**Superior** function … §575 (1923, p. 426)
The more **valued** function … (1923, p. 426)
The **most differentiated** function … §556 (1923, p. 426)
**Orienting** function … §984 (1971)
**Directed** function … §504 (1923, p. 371)
The **decisive** [function] for the **orientation** of **consciousness** … §667 (1923, p. 514)
The **leading** function … (1923, p. 514)
The function of **consciousness** … §694 (1923, p. 532)
**Executive** conscious function … §182 (1923, p. 144)
The **favoured** function … §764 (1923, p. 564)
**Pure** function … §698 … [not to be confused with the psychic mechanisms of

extraversion and introversion] (1923, p. 534)
**Master** §55 (1923, p. 52)
**Independent** function §723 (1923, p. 543)
The **main determining value** §523 (1971)
**Principal determining value** (1923, p. 387)
The **main conscious** function §910 (1928, p. 310)


## Development of one basic psychological function into a typical or independent differentiated function

**159** (1923, p. 377)
The human mind is readily conceived [by empirical science] as a sort of *tabula rasa* [blank slate], that **gradually** gets **covered** with the perceptions and experiences of life. §512

**160** (1923, p. 377)
**From this standpoint** [of empirical science in general] **the idea** [for example] **can be nothing at all *but*** an epiphenomenal, *a posteriori* **abstraction from experiences.** §512

**161** (1923, p. 378)
The **newly-born brain** or function-system is an **ancient instrument**, prepared for quite definite ends; it is *not* only *merely* a passive, apperceptive instrument, ***but*** is ***also*** in active command of experience outside itself, forcing certain conclusions or judgements. §512

**162** (1923, p. 378)
These **adjustments** [to outside experience] are **not merely accidental** or **arbitrary** happenings, but adhere to strictly **preformed conditions**, which are not transmitted through experience, but are *a priori* **conditions of apprehension.** §512

**163** (1923, p. 557)
We are **forced** [based for instance on the evidence of the existence of the four basic psychological types of mental orientation] **to assume**, therefore, that the **given brain-structure** does not owe its **particular nature** *merely* to the **effect** of **surrounding conditions**, *but also and just as much* to the peculiar and autonomous **quality of living matter**, that is, to a fundamental **law of life.** §748

**164** (1923, p. 557)
The given **constitution** of the organism, therefore, is on the one hand a product

26

of **outer conditions**, while on the other it is inherently determined by the **nature of living matter**. §748

**165** (1923, p. 539)
**In this work I employ** the concept of **differentiation chiefly** in respect to **the psychological functions** [thinking, feeling, sensation and intuition]. §705

**166** (1923, p. 539)
**Differentiation** consists in the separation of **the selected function from other functions**, and in the separation of **its individual parts from each other**. §705

**167** (1923, p. 142)
**All psychic functions** [including the four basic functions] are **indistinguishably merged** in the **original** and **fundamental** activity of the psyche [in the unconscious/psychic background]. §180

**168** (1923, p. 539)
**So long as** one function is **still** so **merged with one or more of the other functions** [undifferentiated/undeveloped] as to be quite **unable to appear alone** [in consciousness], it is in an *archaic* state, and therefore **undifferentiated**, that is, it is **not** separated out as a special part from the whole having its own independent existence. §705

**169** (1923, p. 142)
The **lack of differentiation** in the unconscious **arises** in the first place **from** the almost direct **association** of the **brain centres among themselves** [contamination]. §180

**170** (1923, p. 143)
**In the unconscious** the most **heterogeneous elements**, in so far as they possess only a vague analogy, **may become mutually substituted for each other** [applicable also to the four psychological functions]. [For example], even **heterogeneous sense-impressions** coalesce, as we see in colour hearing. §180

**171** (1923, p. 353)
It is always a **delicate matter**, this framing of **physiological or "organic" hypotheses** in connection with **psychological processes**. §479

**172** (1923, p. 619)
Remember, we are here **concerned** only with the **psychological problem**. §846

**173** (1971)
I have given a description of a **purely psychological typology** in my book *Psychological Types*. §970

**174** (1933, p. 106)
Functions [the psychological functions of orientation] are **consciously** brought into **daily use** and are **developed by exercise**. §955

**175** (1923, p. 564)
The very conditions of society enforce a man to **apply** himself **first and foremost** to the **differentiation** of that function with which he is **most gifted by Nature**. §763

**176** (1933, p. 101)
In the struggle for existence and adaptation everyone **instinctively** [through self-regulation of the psyche] uses his **most developed function**. §947

**177** (1923, p. 539-40)
Without differentiation direction is impossible, since the **direction** of a function is **dependent** upon the **isolation and exclusion** of the **irrelevant**. §705

**178** (1923, p. 540)
Through **fusion** with what is irrelevant, direction becomes **impossible**. §705

**179** (1923, p. 540)
**Only** a **differentiated function** [fully differentiated from the other functions] proves itself **capable** of **direction** [thereby establishing a type]. §705

**180** (1923, p. 14)
If one of these functions [thinking, feeling, sensation or intuition] **habitually prevails** [predominates] a **corresponding** [function] **type results**. §7

**181** (1933, p. 101)
The **predominance** of a function leads us to **construct** or to **seek out** certain situations while we **avoid** others, and therefore to have experiences that are **peculiar to us** and **different from those of other people**. §947

**182** (1933, p. 107)
**Whether** a function is **differentiated** or not may easily be **recognised** from its **strength, stability, constancy, trustworthiness,** and *service* in **adaptedness**. §956

**183** (1923, p. 514)

For the sake of clarity let us again **recapitulate**: The **products** of all the functions [irrespective of their quality or the contamination of content] can be **conscious**, but we speak of **the consciousness** [independence] **of a function** only when not merely its application is **at the disposal of the will**, but when at the same time its **principle** is **decisive** for the orientation of consciousness [able to offer differentiated contents habitually]. §667

**184** (1923, p. 14)

I therefore discriminate a thinking, a feeling, a sensation, and an intuitive *type*. §7

## The four independent/superior function-types divide into the rational and irrational pairs of opposites

**185** (1923, p. 612)

The four types may be divided into two classes according to the quality of the respective basic function, namely the *rational* and the *irrational*. §835

## Thinking and feeling: the rational function-types

**186** (1933, p. 103-4)

What I call the **thinking** or **feeling** types embrace two groups of persons who have **something in common** which I cannot designate except by the word *rationality*. §951

**187** (1923, p. 583)

The **rational** is **the reasonable**, that which **accords** with **reason**. §785

**188** (1923, p. 468)

**In so far as the objective occurrence is law-determined**, it is accessible to reason. We apply the term **law-determined** to the **occurrence appearing so** to our **reason**. The **postulate** of a **universal lawfulness** remains a postulate of **reason only**. §616

**189** (1923, p. 584)

*Thinking* and *feeling* attain their **fullest significance** when in **fullest possible accord** with **the laws of reason**. §787

**190** (1933, p. 105)

**Feeling values** and **feeling judgements** – that is to say, our feelings – are not only

**reasonable**, but are also as **discriminating**, **logical** and **consistent** [in accordance with its own principle] as thinking [in accordance with its own principle]. §953

**191** (1923, p. 584)
*Thinking* and *feeling* are rational functions **in so far** as they are **decisively influenced** by the ***motive*** of reflection. §787

## Variant terminologies for the rational function-types

**192**
Rational functions … §787 (1923, p. 584)
Judging functions … §601 (1923, p. 452)
Reasoning functions … §601 (1923, p. 452)
Discriminative functions … §983 (1971)
Functions of rational judgement … §644 (1971)
Reasoning judgement … (1923, p. 495)
[**Thinking and feeling** *equate* **rational functions** *equate* **judging functions** *equate* **reasoning functions** *equate* **discriminative functions** *equate* **functions of rational judgement.**]

## Thinking and feeling: a rational pair of direct opposites

**193** (1971)
**Thinking** [intellectual understanding and conclusions] is **opposed** to **feeling**, because thinking **should not be influenced** or deflected **from its purpose** by feeling values. §983

**194** (1923, p. 514)
**Thinking**, if it is to be real thinking and **true to its own principle**, must **scrupulously exclude** feeling. §667

**195** (1928, p. 308)
**Nothing disturbs** *thinking* **so much** as *feeling*. §905

**196** (1923, p. 514)
**Feeling** in its nature stands in **strong contrast** to thinking. §667

**197** (1933, p. 103)
[Feeling types] conspicuously **neglect** thinking **in favour** of **emotional factors**, that is, feeling. They inveterately **follow** a "**policy**" **dictated** by **feeling**. They form an unmistakable **contrast** to the [thinking] type. §950

**198** (1928, p. 308)
**Nothing** is **more disastrous** to *feeling* than *thinking*. §905


# Sensation and intuition: the irrational function-types

**199** (1971)
**Sensation** and **intuition** I call **irrational**, because they are both **concerned** simply with **what happens** and with **actual** [sensation] or **potential** [intuition] **realities**. §983

**200** (1933, p. 105)
"**What happens**" is essentially **non-rational**. §953

**201** (1923, p. 587)
In so far as **sensation** is an **elementary phenomenon**, it is **something absolutely given**, something that is **not subject to the laws of reason**. §796

**202** (1923, p. 468)
Where the **regularity of an occurrence escapes us** [because we can find no law] we call it **accidental** [not law-determined]. §616

**203** (1923, p. 570)
Sensation and intuition are **concerned** with **accidental perceptions**. §776

**204** (1933, p. 105)
**Sensation and intuition** are simply **receptive** to **what happens**. §953
They **do not act** selectively, **according to principles** [lacking criteria]. §953
Sensation and intuition are **non-rational** [not rational]. §953
Sensation and intuition are **not logical**. §953
Sensation and intuition are **not discriminating**. §953
Sensation and intuition are **not evaluating**. §953
Sensation and intuition do **not interpret**. §953

## Variant terminologies for the irrational function-types

**205**
Irrational functions … §983 (1971)
Functions of perception … §668 (1923, p. 515)
Perceptive functions … §616 (1971)
[**Sensation and intuition** *equate* **irrational functions** *equate* **functions of perception** *equate* **perceptive functions.**]

## Sensation and intuition: an irrational pair of direct opposites

**206** (1933, p. 106)
The **sensation** type is at the **opposite pole** to **the intuitive** [type]. §954

**207** (1923, p. 587)
**Sensation** and **intuition** represent a **pair of opposites.** §795

## The rational versus the irrational function-types

**208** (1923, p. 584)
*Thinking* and *feeling* are **rational functions** in so far as they are **decisively influenced** by the **motive** of reflection. They attain their fullest significance when in **fullest** possible **accord** with the laws of reason. The **irrational functions**, *sensation* and *intuition*, on the contrary, aim at **pure *perception*** [perception of accidentals]. The irrational functions are **forced to dispense with** the rational (which presupposes the **exclusion** of everything that is outside reason) in order to be able to reach the most complete perception of the whole course of events. §787

**209** (1923, p. 569)
In the way that I make use of the term "irrational", it does **not** denote something ***contrary*** to *reason* [not antagonistic to reason], but something ***outside the province*** of reason, whose essence, therefore, is not established by reason. §774

## Decisiveness according to principles versus decisiveness according to the intensity of perception

**210** (1933, p. 105)
When we **think**, it is in order to **judge** or to reach a **conclusion according** to [ob-

jective] **principles**. When we **feel**, it is in order to attach [by way of judgement] a proper value to something **according** to **principles**.

**Sensation** and **intuition** do **not** act selectively, **according to principles**. §953

**211** (1923, p. 428)
**Judgement** always **presupposes** a **criterion**. §577

**212** (1923, p. 468)
I call **sensation** and **intuition** irrational because their *commissions* and *omissions* are **based** [a *priori* decisiveness] not upon reasoned judgement but **upon** the **absolute intensity** of perception. §616

## The four independent/superior function-types as observed in four differentiated individuals, form a dual-axial structure

**213** (1971)
The **four** [superior/independent] **functions** therefore form, when arranged **diagrammatically**, a **cross** with a **rational axis** [thinking and feeling as direct opposites] *at right angles* to an **irrational axis** [sensation and intuition as direct opposites]. §983

**214** (1933, p. 107-8)
The **four functions** are somewhat **like the four points of the compass**. In this way we can orientate ourselves with respect to the immediate world as completely as when we locate a place geographically by latitude and longitude. §958

## Why four superior function-types?

**215** (1933, p. 107)
I have been asked **why** I speak of **four functions** and not of more or fewer. That there are exactly four is a **matter** of **empirical fact**. A certain **completeness** is attained by these four. §958

**216** (1971)
The **differentiation** of the **four orienting functions** is an **empirical consequence** of **typical differences** [one-sidedness] in the **functional attitude** [between individuals]. §984

**217** (1928, p. 305)

These **four fundamental functions** appear to me to be **sufficient** to **express** and **represent** the **ways and means of conscious orientation.** §900

**218** (1923, p. 200)

It would be altogether **unjustifiable** to try to **maintain** that **one type** is in any respect **more valuable** than **the other.** The types are **mutually complementary,** and from **their distinctiveness there proceeds just that measure of tension** which both the **individual** and **society need** for the **maintenance of life.** §264

## The individual has four functions but can develop into only one function-type due to the limited orientation and prejudice of the superior function

**219** (1923, p. 612)

In so far as such an **attitude** [thinking, feeling, sensation or intuition] is *habitual* [predominant], thus lending a **certain stamp** to the character of the individual, I speak of a **psychological type.** §835

**220** (1923, p. 532)

The activity of **consciousness** [the superior function] is ***selective*** [in terms of material and data]. Selection demands ***direction***. But direction requires the **exclusion of everything irrelevant.** §694

**221** (1923, p. 371)

Every **directed function** [for instance thinking] demands the **strict exclusion** of **everything not suited to its nature** [*feelings* and *the irrational*]. Without the repression of everything that differs from itself, the directed function cannot operate at all. §504

**222** (1923, p. 514)

We speak of **the consciousness of a function** [superiority of a function] only when **its application** is **at the disposal of the will,** [and] *at the same time* its **principle** is **decisive for the orientation of consciousness.** §667

**223** (1933, p. 96)

[To repeat], **whatever** we **look at,** and **however** we **look at it, we see *only*** through **our own eyes.** §936

# Inferior function

The term "inferior function" refers to any underdeveloped function whose products are only **variably present in consciousness** and which is still merged with one or more basic functions and can be recognised in the manifestation of its undifferentiated products.

**224** (1923, p. 563)
The term **inferior function** is used to denote the function that **remains** in **arrear** [at the very back] in the process of differentiation. §763

**225** (1928, p. 308-9)
When a function has **not the character of disposability**, when it is **felt as a disturbance of the conscious function** [superior function], when it is moody, **now appearing** and now **vanishing**, when it has an **obsessive character**, or remains **obstinately** in **hiding when most needed** – these qualities are characteristic of a function existing mainly in the unconscious. Such a function has further qualities that are worthy of note; there is something ***un-individual*** about it, that is, **it contains elements which do not necessarily belong to it.** §906

**226** (1933, p. 106)
What happens to **those functions** which are **not developed by exercise** and are not **consciously brought** into **daily use**? They **remain** in a more or less primitive and infantile state, often only **half-conscious** [half-conscious equates half-unconscious], *or even* **quite unconscious.** §955

**227** (1923, p. 102)
It is the **characteristic** of **an imperfectly developed function**, that it **withdraws** itself **from conscious disposition** [conscious control] and with its **own impetus**, that is, with a certain **autonomy**, becomes **unconsciously implicated** with other [imperfectly developed] functions. §118

**228** (1923, p. 135)
On account of its relative repression, the **inferior function** is **only partly attached to consciousness**; its **other part** is **dependent upon the unconscious** [attached to the unconscious]. §171

**229** (1923, p. 539)
**Just so far as** a function is **wholly** or **mainly** unconscious it is also **undifferentiated**. It is ***not only*** **fused together** in its parts ***but also*** **merged with** other functions [contaminated]. §705

**230** (1933, p. 107)
**Inferiority in a function** [insufficiently differentiated] is often not so easily described or recognised. §956

**231** (1933, p. 107)
An **essential criterion** [to recognise inferiority in a function] is its **lack of self-sufficiency**, and our resulting **dependence** on people and circumstances; furthermore, its **disposing** us to moods and undue sensitivity, its **untrustworthiness** and **vagueness**, and its tendency to make us **suggestible**. §956

**232** (1923, p. 539)
The undifferentiated function is also commonly characterised by the qualities of **ambivalence** and **ambitendency**, that is, every positive brings with it an equally strong negative, whereby **characteristic inhibitions** spring up in the application of the undifferentiated function. §705

**233** (1923, p. 100)
The **inferior functions** are **opposed** to the **superior** [principal], **not so much** in their **essential nature** but as a **result** of their **actual momentary** [inferior] **form**. §115

**234** (1933, p. 107)
We are **always** at a **disadvantage** in using the inferior function because we **cannot direct** it, being in fact even its **victims**. §956

**235** (1923, p. 94)
The enslavement of the **inferior functions** [in the grip of unconscious processes] is an **ever-bleeding wound** in the soul of man today. §108

## Each of the four function-types respectively represents a different kind of one-sidedness

**236** (1928, p. 306 & 1933, p. 106)
**Each** of these [four function-] types represents a **different kind of one-sidedness** [in the differentiated individual]. For instance the **one-sided emphasis on** [superior] **thinking is always accompanied** by an **inferiority in feeling**. §901-2 & §955

THUS
One-sided **thinking** is accompanied by **inferior feeling**.
One-sided **feeling** is accompanied by **inferior thinking**.
One-sided **sensation** is accompanied by **inferior intuition**.

One-sided **intuition** is accompanied by **inferior sensation**.

## The unclassifiable – people who lack the development of a principal function

**237** (1923, p. 514-15)
**Uniform consciousness and unconsciousness** of functions is a distinguishing mark of a primitive [underdeveloped] mentality. Individuals certainly exist [for instance] in whom thinking and feeling stand upon the same level. But, in such a case, there is also **no question** of **a differentiated** [thinking or feeling] **type**. §667

**238** (1928, p. 298)
It is the primitive, **un-psychological man**, who regards **affects** [emotions] in himself and others as the **only essential criterion** [thus lacking a superior psychological function]. §887

**239** (1971)
**Affects** can be seen **on the surface**, and that is enough for **the un-psychological man** – the man for whom the psyche of his neighbour presents no problem. He is satisfied with seeing other people's affects; if he sees none, then the other person is psychologically invisible to him because, **apart from affects, he can perceive nothing in the other's consciousness** [due to the undifferentiated "un-problematical" state of his own consciousness]. §885-6

**240** (1928, p. 297)
I call **such a state of consciousness un-problematical**, because it has never been regarded itself as a problem. §886

## Individuals who restrict themselves to the use of only their principal function

**241** (1928, p. 306)
There are **many people** who **restrict** themselves **to** a simple perception of concrete reality [sensation], **without reflecting** much about it, or taking into account the **feeling** values involved. They bother themselves little about the possibilities which lie hidden in a situation [intuition]. **Others** are **exclusively** influenced by what they **think**, and simply cannot adapt themselves to a situation which they cannot comprehend intellectually. **Others** are **guided in everything wholly** by their **feelings**. **Intuitives** [who restrict themselves to the exclusive use of intuition] concern themselves **neither** with [thinking] **ideas nor** with **feeling** reactions, **nor**

yet with the reality of things [sensation], **but give** themselves up **wholly to the lure of possibilities.** §901

**242** (1923, p. 90-91)
The differentiation of **one function** among several inevitably **leads** to **overgrowth** [more pronounced] **of the one** and to **neglect and crippling of the rest.** §105

**243** (1928, p. 308)
**Repressed functions** lapse into the unconscious. Just as, of the four sons of Horus, only one had a human head, so with the four basic functions, **only one** as a rule is fully conscious and **differentiated**, so that it is free and subject to the direction of the will, the other three functions remaining partly or wholly unconscious. By this "unconsciousness" I do not of course mean that an intellectual, for example, would be unconscious of feeling. He knows his feelings very well, in so far as he has any power of introspection, but he gives them **no value** and allows them **no influence. They happen to him**, as it were, **against his intention**; being spontaneous and autonomous [functioning like the instincts], they finally possess themselves of the validity which consciousness denies them [at the cost of the superior function and consciousness]. §905

## An auxiliary function is invariably present and observable in the consciousness of a good few individuals

**244** (1923, p. 513)
Accurate investigation of the individual case **consistently** reveals the fact that, **in conjunction with the most differentiated function**, another function of **secondary importance**, and therefore of **inferior differentiation** [relative to the dominant function] *in* consciousness, is **constantly present**, and is a **relatively determining factor.** §666

**245** (1923, p. 515)
This **auxiliary function** [secondary function] is possible and useful only in so far as it *serves* **the leading function** [dominant function], **without** making **any claim** to **the autonomy of its own principle** [the auxiliary function can never override the principle of the dominant function]. §668

**246** (1923, p. 514)
**Its secondary importance** consists in the fact that, in a given case, it is **not valid in its own right,** as is the primary function, as an absolutely reliable and decisive factor, but **comes into play** more as **an auxiliary** or **complementary function.** §667

**247** (1923, p. 463)

The **auxiliary** as a mere tributary function [to the leading function], is also the instrument which, in the presence of a hopelessly **blocked situation**, works *automatically* **towards the issue,** which no other function could discover the way out of. §612

**248** (1923, p. 516-17)

The secondary function [auxiliary function] **protects** [buffers] **consciousness** [oriented by the principal function] **against the destructive effect of the unconscious** and prepares consciousness to **receive the impact** of the unconscious. §670

**249** (1923, p. 515)

Experience shows that **thinking** as the **primary function** *can* readily **pair with intuition** as the auxiliary function [in one individual], **or** indeed equally well **with sensation** [in another individual], but never with feeling [direct inferior opposite]. §668

THUS

**Principal thinking** can **readily pair** with **intuition or** with **sensation** as the auxiliary in consciousness.

**Principal feeling** can **readily pair** with **intuition or** with **sensation** as the auxiliary in consciousness.

**Principal sensation** can **readily pair** with **thinking or** with **feeling** as the auxiliary in consciousness.

**Principal intuition** can **readily pair** with **thinking or** with **feeling** as the auxiliary in consciousness.

## Summary of the relation between the superior, auxiliary and inferior functions

**250** (1923, p. 437)

The **relative or total unconsciousness** of such tendencies or **functions as are excluded from any participation in the conscious attitude** [the inferior functions are excluded] keeps them in a relative undeveloped state. As compared with **the conscious function** [superior] they are inferior. **To the extent that they are unconscious** [inferior], they become merged with the remaining contents of the unconscious, from which they acquire a **bizarre character. To the extent that they are conscious** [auxiliary], they only play a **secondary role**, although one **of considerable importance** for the whole psychological picture. §588

# SECTION III

## PSYCHIC ENERGY:
## INTROVERSION AND EXTRAVERSION

## The four function-types divide further according to the movement of psychic energy which Jung coined introversion and extraversion or attitude-types

**251** (1923, p. 613)
A **further differentiation** of these function-types, thinking, feeling, sensation and intuition is permitted by the **preferential movements** of the *libido* [psychic energy], namely **introversion** and **extraversion**. §835

**252** (1923, p. 186)
**Introversion** and **extraversion** are to be **distinguished** from the **function-types** as **general basic attitudes**. §248

**253** (1923, p. 613)
A more complete investigation of the material has shown me that **we must treat** the **extraversion** and **introversion** types as **superordinated categories** to the **function-types**. §836

## Psychic energy [libido] and its polarity

**254** (1923, p. 250)
There are **no phenomena** [including psychic phenomena] that are **not energic** [having energy or being energetic]. §337

**255** (1923, p. 250)
Every energic phenomenon *manifests* both beginning and end, above and below, hot and cold, earlier and later, cause and effect, that is, **pairs of opposites**. §337

**256** (1923, p. 571)
In my view **libido** is synonymous with **psychic energy**. Psychic energy is **the intensity of the psychic process**. §778

**257** (1923, p. 250)
**Energy current** necessarily presupposes the existence of an **opposition**, that is, of **two states** of **differing potential**, without which no current can take place. §337

**258** (1923, p. 250)
This **inseparability** of the **energy-concept from** the **concept of opposition** [in other sciences] **also involves** my **libido-concept** [in the psychological realm]. §337

**259** (1923, p. 29)
I spoke of a **splitting** of **libido** into **two halves, each directed against the other**.
§30

**260** (1916, p. 288)
I propose to use the terms **"extraversion"** and **"introversion"** to **describe** these
**two opposite directions of the libido** [pairs of opposites]. §860

**261**
**Extraversion** means an **outward-turning** of *libido*. §710 (1923, p. 542)
[Extraversion is] a **diastolic** [movement of psychic energy]. §6 (1923, p. 12)
[Extraversion is] a **centrifugal movement** of **libido going out**. §878 (1971)

**262**
**Introversion** means a **turning inwards** of the libido. §769 (1923, p. 567)
[Introversion is] a **systolic** [movement of psychic energy]. §6 (1923, p. 12)
[Introversion is] a **centripetal movement** of **libido coming in**. §878 (1971)

**263** (1916, p. 294)
**Extraversion** and **introversion** are **two psychological opposites**. §872

## Consciousness and the unconscious are a pair of polar opposites and each pole corresponds exclusively to either extraversion or introversion

**264** (1923, p. 142)
The whole **nature of consciousness** is **discrimination, distinguishing ego** from
**non-ego**, subject from object, yes from no, and so forth. The **separation into
pairs of opposites** is entirely **due to conscious differentiation**; only consciousness
can recognise the suitable from the unsuitable and worthless. It alone can declare
one function valuable and another worthless, thus **favouring one with the power
of the will** [disposable energy] while **suppressing the claims of the other**. §179

**265** (1923, p. 532)
**Psychologists** often **compare consciousness to the eye**: we speak of a **visual field**
and of a **focal point** of **consciousness**. The nature of consciousness is aptly characterised by this **simile: only a few contents** can attain **the highest grade of consciousness** at the same time, and only a **limited number** of **contents** can be held
at the same time in **the conscious field**. §694

**266** (1923, p. 532)

We know already that the **activity of consciousness** is *selective*. Selection demands *direction*. But **direction** requires the *exclusion* of *everything irrelevant*. On occasion, therefore, a certain **one-sidedness** of the **conscious orientation** is inevitable. §694

**267** (1923, p. 532)

The **contents** that are **excluded** and **inhibited** *by the chosen direction* **sink** into **the unconscious**, where by virtue of their effective existence they form a definite **counter-weight** against the **conscious orientation** [general attitude of consciousness]. The **strengthening** of this counter position **keeps pace** with the **intensification of the conscious one-sidedness** until finally a **noticeable tension** is produced. §694

# Various expressions of the corresponding pair of opposites [consciousness versus the unconscious]

**268**

**Conscious differentiation** versus **the unconscious as the foundations of consciousness**. §179-180 (1923, p. 142)
**Ego** versus **non-ego**. §179 (1923, p. 142)
**Above** versus **below**. §963 (1971)
**Light** versus **darkness**. §964 (1971)
[Ego *equates* conscious differentiation *equates* above *equates* light]
[Non-ego *equates* the unconscious as the foundations of consciousness *equates* below *equates* darkness]

**269** (1923, p. 416)

In our description it will be necessary to **discriminate between** the **conscious** and **unconscious** psychology. §562

**270** (1971)

**Plato** used the **parable** of the **white** and **black horses** to illustrate the **intractability** and **polarity** of the human psyche. §963

**271** (1923, p. 527)

The **presence of two attitudes** is extremely frequent, the **one conscious** and **the other unconscious**. The **conscious attitude has a preparedness of contents** *different* from that of the unconscious, thus a **duality**. §687

## Different attitudes towards the outer world divide human beings into two psychological groups or classes

**272** (1923, p. 416)
*Everyone* is **oriented** by the **data** with which the **outer world provides** him [as it streams into the psyche via the sense organs]. §563

**273** (1923, p. 416)
The **data** supplied by the outside world, **the data** in themselves, are **only relatively decisive.** §563

**274** (1923, p. 472)
The **world** [concrete outer world] exists not merely **in itself**, but also **as it appears** to **me.** §621

**275** (1923, p. 237)
Psychologically, "**the world**" means **how I see** the world, **my attitude** to the world; thus the world can be regarded as "**my will**" and "**my perception**". **In itself the world is indifferent.** It is *my* Yes and No that **create** the **differences.** §322

**276** (1971)
It gradually became clear to me that there must be **two fundamentally different general** [psychological] **attitudes** [to the data from the outside world] which would **divide human** beings into **two groups.** §971

**277** (1971)
 I have **called these two** fundamentally different *attitudes* extraversion and introversion. §972

**278** (1923, p. 412)
The **general types of attitude** are differentiated by their particular **attitude to the object** [thus to the data with which the outside world provides us]. §557

**279** (1923, p. 412)
**General types of attitude** are also **distinguished** by the **direction** of **general interest** or **libido movement.** §556

**280** (1923, p. 9)
I have **termed** the two attitude-types **the *Introversion*** and the ***Extraversion Types*.** §1

**281** (1923, p. 89)

With the **introverted** and **extraverted** *types* I have distinguished **two general classes of men.** §103

**282** (1923, p. 12)

The **psychology resulting** from **these antagonistic standpoints** must be distinguished as two **totally different orientations.** §5

**283** (1923, p. 12)

It is **not easy** to **characterise** this **contrasting relationship to the object** in a way that is **lucid** and intelligible. §5

# Different focal points

Expressed in terms of the simile of the eye, when data of the same object or event in the outside world confronts the extravert and introvert, their conscious attitude orientates them in opposite directions and towards different focal points.

# The focal point of consciousness in the extravert

**284** (1923, p. 417)

The **extravert's entire consciousness looks outwards** to the world, because the important and decisive determination [for the extravert] **always** comes from without. §563

**285** (1923, p. 11)

The **fundamental idea** of **extraversion** is an **outward movement** of **interest** towards the **object.** §4

**286** (1923, p. 228)

The **extraverted consciousness** is seeking a relation **to the real world** [the outer world or outer reality or concrete reality]. §310

**287** (1923, p. 471)

The **extravert** is prevailingly **orientated by the object** [concrete object] and **objective data.** §620

**288** (1923, p. 412)

The **extravert** maintains a **positive relation** to the object [the concrete or outer object]. §557

**289** (1923, p. 116)
The **extravert** lays much more **stress** upon the **continuity** of the **relation** with **the object**. §138

**290** (1923, p. 116)
Extraversion involves a **differentiation** of **the relation to the object**. §238

**291** (1923, p. 130)
The extravert **finds** himself **through** the **object** [concrete object]. §164

**292** (1923, p. 11)
The **outer object** works **like a magnet** upon the tendencies of the extravert subject; therefore, the object is an attraction that **determines the extravert subject** to a large extent. §4

**293** (1923, p. 412)
The object can **never** have **sufficient value** for the extravert. The importance of the object must always be paramount. §557

**294** (1923, p. 417)
The **extravert's interest** and **attention follow objective happenings** and, **primarily**, those of the **immediate environment**. §563

**295** (1923, p. 116)
The extravert **reveals** himself **simply** and **solely** in his **relation to the object**. §138

**296** (1923, p. 12)
The **extravert sees everything** from the view-point of **the objective occurrence**. §5

**297** (1923, p. 472)
The **extraverted type refers *primarily*** to that which reaches him from the object. §621

**298** (1923, p. 417)
The **objective determinant always wins** in the end [for the extravert]. §563

**299** (1923, p. 417)
When the **orientation to the object** and to **objective facts** is so **predominant** that the most essential **decisions are determined** by **objective relations**, one speaks of an extraverted attitude. §563

# Limitations of the conscious orientation
# of extraverts

**300** (1923, p. 423)
A **purely** [external] **objective orientation** does **violence** to a multitude of **subjective emotions, intentions, needs,** and **desires**, since it robs them of the psychic energy which is their natural right. §570

**301** (1923, p. 473)
Through an **overvaluation** of the **objective powers** of **cognition** [cognition of the external object], we **repress** the importance of the **subjective factor**, which simply means the **denial of the subject**. §621

**302** (1923, p. 473)
But **what is the subject?** The subject is **man – we are the subject**. §621

**303** (1923, p. 473)
**Cognition must have a subject.** There exists for us **no knowledge** and no world **unless "I know"** has been said. §621

**304** (1923, p. 420)
The **extravert's danger** is that he becomes **caught up in objects** and wholly **loses himself in their toils**. §565

**305** (1923, p. 412)
The **extravert** *affirms* the **importance** of the **object** *to such an extent* that his **subjective attitude** [ego-attitude] is **continually being orientated** *by*, and **related** *to* the **object**. §557

**306** (1923, p. 422)
It seems that the **extraverted type** is *constantly tempted* to give himself as subject **away** in **favour of the object**. §569

**307** (1923, p. 422)
The **extraverted type** is *constantly tempted* to **assimilate his subject** [ego-consciousness] *to* the **object**. §569

**308** (1923, p. 417)
He **naturally** has **subjective views, but** their **determining power** has **less importance than** the external **objective conditions**. §563

**309** (1923, p. 417)

**Therefore**, the extraverted subject **never expects** to find any ***absolute factors*** in his own inner life, since **the only ones** he knows are **outside himself** [relating to the external object]. §563

**310** (1923, p. 418)

**Objective occurrences** have a well-nigh **inexhaustible charm**, so that in the normal course the extravert's interest **makes no other claims** [for a subjective factor]. §563

**311** (1923, p. 494)

**An extraverted consciousness** is **unable** to believe in **invisible forces** [in the non-concrete or abstract]. §641

## The focal point of consciousness in the introvert

**312** (1923, p. 472)

**Perception and cognition** are not purely objective: they are also **subjectively conditioned**. §621

**313** (1923, p. 11)

The **fundamental idea** of **introversion** is a **movement** of **interest away from** the **object** towards the **subject** and **his own psychological processes**. §4

**314** (1923, p. 12)

The **introverted standpoint** is one that under all circumstances ***sets* the self** and the **subjective psychological process** *above* the **object and the objective process**, or at any rate ***holds its ground against*** the object. §5

**315** (1923, p. 12)

The **introverted consciousness** *selects* the **subjective determinants** as the **decisive** ones. §621

**316** (1923, p. 471)

The **introvert** is ***governed*** by **subjective factors**. §620

**317** (1923, p. 473)

We must be quite clear as to what meaning the term "**subjective**" carries in this investigation. §622

**318** (1923, p. 473)

By the **subjective factor**, then, I understand that **psychological action** or reaction which, when merged with the **effect of the** [outer] **object** [on the consciousness of the introvert], makes **a new psychic fact**. §622

**319** (1923, p. 472)
The introvert principally **relies upon that which** the outer impression **constellates in the subject**. §621

**320** (1923, p. 472)
The introverted consciousness is **guided** by **that factor** of **perception and cognition** [abstract image or subjective factor] **which represents** the receiving **subjective disposition** [the introverted response] to the sense stimulus [what the sense impression constellates in the subject]. §621

**321** (1923, p. 476)
The **contents of the collective unconscious** are **represented** [constellated] **in consciousness** [in the introvert's consciousness] in the form of **pronounced tendencies**, or **definite ways of looking at things**. They are generally regarded by the individual as being determined by the [outer] object – incorrectly, at bottom – since **they have their source in the unconscious structure of the psyche**, and are only **released** by the **operation of the object**. §625

**322** (1923, p. 475)
The **introverted attitude** is normally **governed** by the **psychological structure**, theoretically determined by heredity, but which to the [introverted] subject is an ever present subjective factor. This must not be assumed to be simply identical with the subject's ego. It is the **psychological structure** of the subject that **precedes any development of the ego**. §623

**323** (1923, p. 475)
The **psychological structure** is what I call the "**collective unconscious**". *The individual* self is a **portion**, or **excerpt**, or **representative of something universally present in all living creatures**, and, therefore, a correspondingly graduated kind of psychological process, which is **born anew in every creature**. §624

**324** (1923, p. 211)
The **collective unconscious**, regarded as the **historical background** of the **psyche**, **contains** in a **concentrated form** the **entire succession of engrams** (imprints), which **from time immemorial** have **determined** the **psychic structure as it now exists**. §281

**325** (1923, p. 423)
Man **bears** his **age-long history** [his subjective impulses, intentions, needs and

desires] with him; in his very **structure** is written the **history of mankind.** The **historical factor** represents a ***vital need***, to which a wise psychic economy ***must*** respond. Somehow **the past *must*** become **vocal**, and **participate in the present.** §570

**326** (1923, p. 417)
The introvert **reserves a view** which is **interposed** between **himself** and **the objective fact.** §563

**327** (1923, p. 471)
The introvert ***interposes*** a **subjective view** [*a priori* to action] between the **perception of the object** and his **own action**, which **prevents** the action from assuming a **character** that **corresponds** with the **objective situation.** §620

**328** (1923, p. 11-12)
In the case of the introvert **the subject** is and remains **the centre of every interest.** It looks as though all the life-energy were ultimately **seeking the subject.** It is as though energy were flowing away **from the** [external] **object**, as if **the subject** were a **magnet** which would draw the object **to itself.** §4

**329** (1923, p. 476)
The **subjective** tendencies and ideas are **stronger** than **the objective influence** [for introverts]; because their **psychic value** is higher, they are **superimposed upon all impressions.** §625

**330** (1923, p. 472)
**Introverted consciousness** doubtlessly views the **external conditions**, but it **selects** the **subjective determinants** as the **decisive ones.** §621

**331** (1923, p. 472)
Introversion means a **turning inward** of the **libido** whereby a **negative relation** of **subject** to **object** is expressed. §769

**332** (1923, p. 12)
The **introvert sees everything** [in the outside world] **from the angle of his conception.** §5

**333** (1923, p. 473)
**Elementary perceptions** and **cognitions** are almost **universally** the **same.** In so far as the **subjective factor, since oldest times** and **among all peoples**, remains in a very large measure **identical with itself**, the **subjective factor is a reality** that is **just as firmly established** as the **outer object.** §622

**334** (1923, p. 473-4)

**If this were not so**, any sort of **permanent** and **essentially changeless reality** would be altogether **inconceivable**. §622

**335** (1923, p. 474)

The **subjective factor** is something that is **just as much a fact** as the extent of the sea and the radius of the earth. The subjective factor claims **the whole value of a world-determining power** which can never, under any circumstances, be excluded from our calculations. §622

**336** (1923, p. 474)

The subjective factor is **the other world-law**, and the man who is **based** upon it has a **foundation just as secure, permanent,** and **valid** *as the man* who relies **upon the object**. §622

**337** (1923, p. 412)

The **introvert's attitude** to the [external] object is *an abstracting one*. §557

**338** (1923, p. 521)

When I assume *an abstracting attitude* towards an [outer] **object, I do not let** *the object* affect me in its totality, but **I distinguish a portion** of it from its connections, at the same time excluding the irrelevant parts. My **purpose** is to **rid myself** of **the object as a single and unique whole**, and to **extract** *only* a portion of it. **Awareness** of the whole undoubtedly takes place, but **I do not plunge myself into this awareness; my interest** does not flow out into the totality, but **withdraws itself from the object as a whole, bringing the abstracted portion into myself,** that is, **into my** [subjective] **world**, which is already prepared [through psychic self-regulation] or **constellated** for the **purpose** of abstracting *a part of the object*. §679

**339** (1923, p. 520)

**Abstraction** is the drawing out or **isolation of a content** (a meaning or general characteristic, etc.) **from a connection, containing other elements,** whose **combination as a totality is something unique or individual** [given the immediate conditions of time and place], and therefore inaccessible to comparison [thus with the surplus elements of the said content]. §676

**340** (1923, p. 520)

**Abstraction** is that form of **mental activity** [in the introverted type] which **releases the essential content or fact** from its connection **with irrelevant elements;**

it distinguishes it from them. In its wider sense, **everything is *abstract*** that is **separated from its connection** with **non-appertaining elements**. §677

**341** (1923, p. 476)
Therefore, the **introvert** has a **highly generalised mode of expression**. §625

**342** (1923, p. 522)
I call an **attitude abstracting** when it is *both* introverting and *at the same time* assimilates to already prepared abstract contents in the subject a certain essential portion of the object. §680

**343** (1923, p. 567)
When **introversion** is **habitual** [predominant], one speaks of an *introverted* type. §769

## Limitations of the conscious orientation of introverts

**344** (1923, p. 477)
The **superior position** of the **subjective factor** in consciousness [the introverted consciousness] involves an **inferiority** of the **objective factor** [concrete outer object]. The object is **not given** that **importance** which should really belong to it. The object has **too little to say** in the introvert. §626

**345** (1923, p. 477)
**To the extent** that the introvert's **consciousness** is **subjectified**, the **object** [outer reality] is placed in a **position** which in time becomes quite **untenable**. §626

## Extraversion and introversion are psychic mechanisms

**346** (1923, p. 354)
**Extraversion** and **introversion** are **not** [about] **character** at all, **but *mechanisms***. §479

**347** (1923, p. 12-13)
Extraversion and introversion are **merely** opposite **mechanisms** – a **diastolic** going out and **seizing** of the **object**, and a **systolic concentration** and **release** of energy **from the object seized** [concrete outer object]. §6

**348** (1916, p. 292)
The **diversity** of extraversion and introversion is **the result of** a different **localisa-**

tion of the **libido** [localised in two different focal points of consciousness]. In the **extravert** *libido* is directed to the objective world [outer focal point]. In the introvert *libido* is directed towards the internal life [inner focal point or subjective factor]. §869

## Our psyches are polar

**349** (1923, p. 12)
**Extraversion** and **introversion** are **opposite mechanisms**. §6

**350** (1923, p. 10)
**Every individual** possesses both mechanisms [in the individual's psyche as a whole], **extraversion** *as well as* **introversion**. §4

**351** (1923, p. 13)
There can **never** occur a **pure type** *in the sense* that he is entirely possessed of the **one mechanism** [unipolar] with **complete atrophy** of **the other**. §6

**352** (1971)
Extraversion and introversion [irrespective which of the two is predominant] are **two modes** of **psychic reaction** [diastolic and systolic] which can be **observed** in **the same individual**. §862

## The unconscious of the extravert is introverted and the unconscious of the introvert is extraverted

**353** (1923, p. 496)
**Extraversion** and **introversion exclude each other** and they **cannot possibly exist** *side by side*. §644

**354** (1923, p. 228)
The **conscious** has **two attitudes** – the **Promethean**, which withdraws the libido **from the world**, introverting **without giving out**, and the **Epimethean**, which is **constantly responding** [giving out], held [captivated] by the claims of external objects. §310

**355** (1928, p. 310)
The qualities of the **conscious attitude** are in **strict contrast** to those of the qualities of the **unconscious attitude**. We can say that **between** the **conscious attitude**

and **the unconscious** there is normally an **opposition**. §910

**356** (1928, p. 306)
Investigation of the unconscious has revealed the fact that, in the case of an **introvert** [conscious introversion] there exists **alongside**, or rather **behind** his **conscious attitude**, an ***unconscious extraverted attitude*** [unconscious extraversion]. §902

**357** (1923, p. 228)
If the **attitude** is mainly **introverted** and given to **abstraction**, the **extraverted** function [the unconscious] is ***inferior***. §310

**358** (1928, p. 306)
Investigation of the unconscious has revealed the fact that, in the case of an **extravert** [conscious extraversion] there exists **alongside**, or rather **behind** his **conscious attitude**, an ***unconscious introverted attitude*** [unconscious introversion]. §902

**359**
There are thus **two forms** of **inferiority**:
***Inferior*** extraversion and ***inferior*** introversion. §879 (1971)
***Repressed*** extraversion [unconscious extraversion] in the **introvert**. §93 (1923, p. 82)
***Repressed*** introversion [unconscious introversion] in the **extravert**. §93 (1923, p. 82)

# Psychic energy flows along the gradient between the opposite poles of consciousness and the unconscious

**360** (1923, p. 250)
As already mentioned, the **concept** of **opposition** is also associated with the **energy-concept**. An energy current necessarily ***presupposes*** the existence of **two states of differing potential**, without which no current can take place. §337

**361** (1923, p. 261-2)
**Libido** as a **psychological energy concept** corresponds with the attribute of a **determined, regulated process;** since a process ***always*** proceeds from a ***higher*** potential to a ***lower***. §355

**362** (1971)
We find a **very valuable parallel** to **extraversion** and **introversion** [that sheds light on the flow of psychic energy between the two poles of consciousness and the unconscious] in the theory of **Wilhelm Worringer**, who speaks of **empathy** and **abstraction**. §871

**363** (1971)
[Worringer's term] "**empathy**" corresponds to the **mechanism of extraversion**, and [his term] "**abstraction**" to the **mechanism of introversion**. §493

**364** (1923, p. 362)
**Introversion** as a **conscious act** of **abstraction** is ***preceded*** by an **unconscious** act of **projection** [empathy or inferior extraversion]. §490

**365** (1923, p. 362-3)
In this unconscious act of projection, **negatively stressed contents** are **transferred** to the object [thereby creating a higher potential in the concrete outer object and a lower potential in the introvert subject]. §490-1

**366** (1971)
The abstracting **introverted attitude** ***endows*** the **object** [due to unconscious extraversion] with a **threatening** or injurious **quality** against which it has to **defend** itself. §490

**367** (1923, p. 363)
The man with the abstracting attitude [the introvert] finds himself in a **terribly animated** [concrete outer] **world**, which seeks to **overpower** and smother him. §492

**368** (1923, p. 362)
**Abstraction** [introversion] ***presupposes*** a certain **living and operating force** on the part of **the object** [having a higher energy value than the subject due to unconscious extraversion]; hence it seeks to **remove** itself from the **object's influence** [by orienting towards the subjective factor that interposes itself between subject and outer animated object]. §490

**369** (1971)
**Faced** with the bewildering profusion of animated objects, the **introvert creates** an abstraction, **an abstract universal image** which **conjures** the **welter of impressions** into a **fixed form**. §499

**370** (1923, p. 368)
The **introverted type** becomes so lost and **submerged** in this **abstract image** that finally its **abstract truth** is *set above* the reality of life. §499

**371** (1923, p. 368)
In this way he divests himself of his real self and **transfers** his life **into his abstraction**, in which it is, so to speak, **crystallised**. §499

**372** (1923, p. 362)
Since **introversion** is **preceded** by *unconscious extraversion*, **we may** reasonably **ask** whether **extraversion may** not also be **preceded** by an *unconscious introversion*. §491

**373** (1923, p. 362)
Since extraversion, like introversion, is a conscious act, and **since introversion** is **preceded** by an **unconscious projection**, we may **reasonably ask whether extraversion** may not also be **preceded** by an **unconscious act**. §491

**374** (1923, p. 362-3)
**Since** the **nature of extraversion** is a **projection** of subjective contents **into the object**, the antecedent **unconscious act** [for extraversion] must be the **opposite than with introversion**, thus [inferior] **unconscious abstract creations**. §491-2

**375** (1923, p. 362-3)
In this way the **object** is **emptied**, robbed of its spontaneity, and thereby **made a suitable receptacle** for **subjective contents** [projected from the extraverted subject]. §491

**376** (1923, p. 362 & 366)
This unconscious neutralising of the outer **object** [through inferior introversion], that precedes extraversion, **gives the object** a **permanently** *lower energy value*. §491 & 497

**377** (1923, p. 366)
In the case of **extraversion** one might speak of a **continually** unconscious abstraction. §497

**378** (1923, p. 363)
**Only by such means can that difference of potential arise** which the act of extraversion demands for the subjective contents to be conveyed into the object. §491

**379** (1923, p. 368)

The extravert type yields himself **to** the object. He **becomes** the object and in this way gets **rid of himself**. Because he objectifies himself, he **de-subjectifies** himself. §500

**380** (1923, p. 369)

**Extraversion** is a **defence** against the **disintegration caused by inner subjective factors** [unconscious introversion]. §501

## Attitude-types are inborn

**381** (1923, p. 413-4)

The **extraverted** and **introverted types** have, apparently, quite **a random distribution**. In the **same family** *one child* is extraverted, and *another* introverted. §558

**382** (1923, p. 414)

Since, in the light of these **facts, the attitude-type** [extraversion and introversion] regarded as a **general phenomenon** having an apparently random distribution, **can be no** affair of **conscious intention**, its existence **must be due** to some *unconscious, instinctive cause*. §558

**383** (1923, p. 414)

**Extraversion** and **introversion**, as two **psychological modes of adaptation** [contra biological adaptation] must therefore in some way or other have its *biological precursor*. **At this point a mere general indication must suffice** [regarding a biological foundation underlying the purely psychological attitude-types]. §558-9

**384** (1923, p. 354)

There is an undoubted **predilection** depending upon a certain **inborn disposition**. §479

## Summary of the two attitude-types

**385** (1923, p. 472)

The **extraverted type** *refers* pre-eminently to **that which reaches him from the object**, the **introverted type** principally *relies* upon **that which the outer impression constellates in the subject** [having different focal points of consciousness]. *In an individual case* of apperception, the **difference** may, of course, be very **delicate, but in the total psychological economy** it is **extremely noticeable**. An extravert and introvert see the same object, but they never see it in such a way as to receive two identically similar images of it. §621

## Tension between extraverts and introverts

**386** (1928, p. 304)

It is a sad, but none the less frequent occurrence that the **two types** are inclined to **depreciate each other**. This is due to the fact that the psychic values have a completely opposite accent in the two types. The introvert sees all that holds value for him in the subject, while the extravert sees it in the object. But this dependence upon the object appears to the introvert as a great inferiority, while to the extravert the inferior condition lies in an unmitigated subjectivity. He can see nothing in such an attitude but infantile auto-eroticism. §898

# SECTION IV

## FUNCTION-TYPES AND PSYCHIC ENERGY: A CRITICAL RELATION

# A purely psychological typology

**387** (1923, p. 412)
***The general attitude-types*** I have termed ***extraverted*** and ***introverted***. The two general **attitude-types**, as I have pointed out more than once, are **differentiated** by their particular ***attitude to the object***. The introvert's attitude to the external object is an abstracting one. The extravert, on the contrary, maintains a positive relation to the object. The extravert affirms the importance of the object to such an extent that his subjective attitude is continually being orientated by, and related to, the object. §556-7

**388** (1923, p. 412)
In addition to the attitude-types, there are ***the more special types***. I call them ***the function-types*** [thinking, feeling, sensation and intuition]. The **particularity** of the **four function-types** is due to the fact that **the individual's most differentiated function** plays the principal role in their adaptation or orientation to life. §556

**389** (1923, p. 13-14)
**Individuals** can thus be **differentiated** not only by the universal difference of **extraversion** and **introversion**, but also according to individual **basic psychological functions**. §7

# Psychic energy cannot be observed except in its manifestations

**390** (1923, p. 13-14)
**Psychic energy** [extraversion and introversion] is ***manifested*** in **definite psychic operations** ("effects"). §778

# It is easy to recognise extraversion and introversion in their general manifestations but complicated to make a scientific diagnosis of a type

**391** (1933, p. 98)
***Little* is gained** with the terms **extraversion** and **introversion** in themselves. §938

**392** (1923, p. 167-8)
Our two mechanisms are **basic phenomena** of **a rather general nature**, which

only **vaguely** outline the specific. §219

**393** (1933, p. 99)
The **contrast** between **extraversion** and **introversion** is **simple enough,** *but* simple formulations are unfortunately most **open to doubt.** They all too easily **cover up** the **actual complexities**, and so deceive us. §943

**394** (1928, p. 302)
Although **there are** doubtless certain **individuals** in whom one can recognise the [attitude-] **type** at a **first glance** [by the experienced investigator], this is *by no means always the case*. §895

**395** (1928, p. 309-10)
The outside **observer** sees the **manifestations of the conscious attitude**, as well as the **autonomous phenomena of the unconscious**, and he will be uncertain as to **what he should ascribe** *to the conscious* and what *to the unconscious*. §909

**396** (1928, p. 302-3)
**However clear** and **simple** the **fundamental principle** of the opposing attitudes may be, their **concrete reality** is none the less *complicated* and *obscure*. §895

**397** (1933, p. 99)
**Extraversion** and **introversion** attain **meaning** and **value** *only* when we **realise** [have observed] all the other [typological] **characteristics** [through their manifestations] that go with the type. §938

**398** (1923, p. 11)
The **existence** of the said **two attitude-types** is a **fact** that **has long been known.** §4

**399** (1923, p. 11)
The **names** and **forms** in which **the mechanism of extraversion** and **introversion** have been **conceived** by the observer of human nature are **extremely diverse.** This mechanism **presented** itself **for example** to Goethe's *intuition* as the embracing principle of *diastole* and *systole*. §4

**400** (1928, p. 307)
**In practice** one can surmise *intuitively* the existence of an **extraverted** or **introverted** attitude in general, **but** an *exact scientific investigation* cannot content itself with an *intuition*. §903

**401** (1933, p. 100)
As pointed out before, no sound **criteria** are to be found in the chaos of contemporary psychology. **They have first to be made** – not out of whole cloth, of course, but on the basis of the invaluable preparatory work done by many men. §946

**402** (1933, p. 96)
**Science** is never made by one man. §936

## The four function-types are linked to and complicated by the two attitude-types

**403** (1928, p. 306)
**Each** one of the four **function-types** [thinking, feeling, sensation and intuition] is **complicated** *in a peculiar way* with the generally **extraverted** and **introverted** attitudes. §902

## Only differentiated individuals can be classified

**404** (1971)
The **difference** of **attitude** between **extraversion** and **introversion** becomes **plainly observable only** when we are confronted with a comparatively **well-differentiated** personality [conscious individual]. §971

## Only the psychological types in consciousness can be classified

**405** (1923, p. 526-7)
The **extraverted** and **introverted attitudes** always have an **objective** [focal point]; this can be *either* **conscious** *or* **unconscious**. §687

**406** (1923, p. 453-4)
As previously stressed, I **base my presentation** [of material and classification] *on the* subjective *conscious psychology of the individual*, since **there**, at least, **one has** a **definite** *objective* **footing** [empirical footing]. This footing completely drops away the moment we try to ground psychological principles upon the unconscious. §601

## Extraversion and introversion modify thinking, feeling, sensation and intuition in definite ways

**407** (1923, p. 421)
The **basic psychological functions** [the four function-types] undergo ***modifications* as a result of the general attitude of consciousness** in the extravert [likewise in the case of introverts]. §567

**408** (1933, p. 103)
A man may give preference for instance to thinking whether he be extraverted or introverted, but he **always** uses it **in the way** that is **characteristic** of his **attitude-type**, thus of extraversion or introversion. §950

**409** (1923, p. 498)
Another example is **sensation** which undergoes a considerable **modification** in the **introverted attitude**. §647

**410** (1923, p. 428-434)
See for instance the **description** of the **modification** of thinking through extraversion in *Psychological Types*, par. 577-583

**411** (1923, p. 498-500)
See for example also the **description** of the **modification** of sensation through introversion in *Psychological Types*, par. 647-49.

## The sole criterion for extraversion and introversion

**412** (1928, p. 307)
No person is simply **extraverted** or **introverted**, but he is so **in the form of certain functions** [thinking, feeling, sensation or intuition]. §903

**413** (1928, p. 311)
I would like to stress that each of the two attitudes **extraversion** and **introversion** *appears* in the individual **through** a special kind of **predominance of one of the four basic functions** [thinking, feeling, sensation or intuition]. §913

**414** (1933, p. 101)
Everyone **instinctively** uses his **most developed function** [extraverted or introverted thinking, feeling, sensation or intuition], which thus becomes the ***criterion*** of his **habitual reactions**. §947

## The four function-types are the only criteria for classifying extraverts and introverts

**415** (1928, p. 307)
I must again mention the function-types [thinking, feeling, sensation and intuition]. In **individual cases** the **extraverted** and **introverted attitudes** can never be demonstrated as existing *per se*. They **appear** as the **characteristics** of the **dominating conscious functions**. §903

**416** (1933, p. 101)
An introvert does **not simply** draw back and hesitate before the object, **but** he does so **in a quite definite way**. Just as the lion strikes down his enemy or his prey with his fore-paw, in which his strength resides, and not with his tail like the crocodile, so our **habitual** [psychological] **reactions** are normally **characterised** by the application of our **most trustworthy** and **efficient function**; it is an expression of our strength. §947

**417** (1923, p. 613)
A **differentiation** of the four **function-types** into two classes is permitted **by the preferential movements of the libido**, namely extraversion and introversion. §835

**418** (1928, p. 307)
No person is simply **extraverted** or **introverted**, but he is so **in the form of certain functions** [dominant and auxiliary if differentiated]. §903

**419** (1928, p. 311-12)
**Strictly speaking** [scientifically], there are in reality **no unqualified extraverts** or **introverts**, **but extraverted and introverted function-types**, such as thinking types, sensation types, etc. §913

**420** (1928, p. 307)
Let us take for example **an intellectual** [thinking] type. We must interpret *the nature of his general attitude* [extraversion or introversion] **from** the **peculiarity** of the ***conscious material*** which ***he presents*** to observation. §903

**421** (1971)
**In practice** these four function-types are always **combined** with the attitude-type, that is, with extraversion or introversion, so that the **functions *appear*** in an extraverted or introverted variation. §985

**422** (German, 1936, p. 271)
From this arises an arrangement of **eight** practically demonstrable **function-types**. §985.

**423** (1928, p. 312)
Thus there arise a **minimum** of eight **clearly distinguishable** types [extravert and introvert thinking, feeling, sensation and intuition]. §913

## In every respect

**424** (1933, p. 98)
One cannot be **introverted** or **extraverted** without being so *in every respect*. By the term "introverted" we mean that all psychic happenings take place in the way we posit as true of introverted people. Thus also, to establish [merely] the fact that a certain individual is extraverted would be irrelevant as proving that his height is six feet. §939

**425** (1928, p. 310)
It is sufficiently clear that **the qualities of the main conscious function** [the criterion for extraversion and introversion as a whole], *that is*, **the qualities of the general conscious attitude**, are in strict contrast to the qualities of the unconscious attitude. §910

**426** (1928, p. 311)
The **conscious attitude** is always **in the nature** of a **philosophy of life** [world-view], when it is not definitely a religion. §911

**427** (1923, p. 528)
The **total psychology** of the individual even in its various basic characters is **orientated** by the nature of his **habitual attitude** [extraversion or introversion]. §690

**428** (1923, p. 613)
The **differentiation** into rational and irrational function-types [*Magna Carta*, section II] **has nothing to do with** extraversion and introversion. §835

**429** (1933, p. 99)
**Extraversion *or* introversion**, as a typical attitude, means **an essential bias** which conditions the whole psychic process. It also denotes the kind of compensatory activity of the unconscious which we may expect to find. §940

**430** (1923, p. 88)

A person who belongs to **a definite type** [for instance thinking], is therefore **constrained**, even in spite of himself, **to deliver a one-sided characterisation** of his ideas [thinking]. This is nowhere so apparent as in psychological presentations, where it is **almost impossible** for us to trace any other picture than that whose main outlines are already marked out in our own psyche. §102

## A critical methodology for classifying an individual

**431** (1971)

The purpose of a psychological typology is to provide a critical psychology that will make a ***methodical*** investigation and **presentation of the empirical material** possible. §986

**432** (1923, p. 17)

When **the observer** [the one who classifies] is **adequately informed** concerning **the compass** [orientation] **and nature** of his **own personality,** the **basic condition for the scientific and accurate estimation** [classification] of *a psyche* **differing from that of the observing subject** [conscious psyche of the individual being classified], is **fulfilled.** §11

**433** (1923, p. 17)

The observer can be sufficiently informed [about the nature of his own personality] only when he has in great measure **freed himself** from the **compromising influence** of **collective opinion** and feeling, and has thereby **reached** a **clear conception** of **his own individuality.** §11

**434** (1971)

The **practising psychologist** can **avoid** many serious **blunders** in dealing with his patients when **armed** with an **exact knowledge** of his own differentiated and inferior **functions.** §986

**435** (1928, p. 307)

An exact scientific investigation must concern itself with **the actual material presented** [by the individual]. Let us take **for example** a ***thinking type***; most of **the conscious material which he presents to observation** consists of thoughts, conclusions, deliberations, as well as actions, affects [instinctive], feeling valuations [inferior unconscious disturbances], and perceptions of an intellectual nature.

We must **interpret** *the essence of his general attitude* from the **peculiarity** of this **material**. The **material** presented by a feeling type will be of a different kind. Only **from the peculiar nature** of his feelings shall we be able to tell to which of the attitude-types he belongs. §903

**436** (1923, p. 88)
**From various characteristics** [based on an individual's actual words], a ***conclusion*** can be made **as to the type**, by tracing the identification of **the individual** with **their own image** [own viewpoint] **in their description** [for example in written material], and **the limitations imposed thereby upon their formulations**. This limitation is to be ascribed to the fact that the one mechanism [the general attitude of consciousness] is presented in richer outline than the other [the attitude of the unconscious], for the latter is still imperfectly developed, and must necessarily have certain inferior characters clinging to it. §103

**437** (1928, p. 310)
A **differential diagnosis** can only be founded on a **careful study** of the **material**. §909

**438** (1928, p. 310)
We must try to **discover** which phenomena proceed from **consciously chosen motives** and which are **spontaneous** [instinctive]. We must also determine which manifestations possess an **adapted**, and which an **unadapted**, archaic [infantile] character. §909

**439** (1933, p. 94)
The particular variations are certainly as innumerable as the **variations of crystals** which nevertheless may be **recognised as belonging to one or another system**. But just as crystals show **basic uniformities** which are relatively simple, so do these **personal attitudes** show certain **fundamental traits** which allow us to assign them to **definite groups**. §932

# An exact classification

**440** (1928, p. 296)
In the **earlier centuries**, when the concept "psychology" as we know it today was almost entirely lacking, the four **function-types** were **veiled in obscurity**; as indeed to the great majority of people today they seem to be scarcely discernible subtleties. §885

**441** (1928, p. 298)

**Only** when an individual has produced a **discrimination between various psychological factors in himself**, is he in a position to summon other criteria in his psychological judgement of others. **Only in this way** is the development of a really *objective psychological critique* possible. §887

**442** (1971)

In a science as young as psychology, **limiting definitions** will sooner or later become an **unavoidable necessity**. In the future psychologists will have to agree upon certain basic principles **secure from arbitrary interpretation** if psychology is not to remain an unscientific and fortuitous conglomeration of individual opinions. §987

**443** (German, 1936, p. 272)

The proposal I put forward, a practical experience-based typological system, is **an attempt to provide a basis** and **a framework** for the unlimited individual variations that have prevailed until now **in the formation of psychological perceptions** [views]. §987

**444** (1923. p. 519)

In the **domain of psychology** we are [scientifically] **dependent** on the **precision of the concept**. §673

**445** (1923, p. 519-617)

We can now understand that the **individual pioneer** must at least strive to give his concepts some **fixity** and **precision**; and this is best achieved by so elucidating **the meaning of the concepts** he employs as to put everyone in a position to see what he means by them. §674-844 [Definitions]

**446** (1928, p. 302)

As a rule, *only* **careful observation** and **weighing** of the **evidence permit a** *sure classification*. §895

**447** (1923, p. 621)

I hope that through a **consideration** of the problem of typical attitudes, and the **presentation** of it in a **certain form and outline** [thinking form], I may **contribute** a small share to the **knowledge** of the almost infinite variations and gradations of **individual psychology**. §848

## *Psychological Types* is the first and only purely psychological typology

**448** (1933, p. 93)
A **decision** is something of a *purely* psychic nature. §930

**449** (1923, p. 530)
Typical thinking, feeling, sensation and intuition are *purely* psychological attitude-types. §691

**450** (1971)
See my **detailed** description of a *purely* psychological typology in my book *Psychological Types*. §970

## *Psychological Types* is a critical tool

**451** (1971)
The **purpose** of a psychological typology is to provide a *critical psychology* [relating to objective rational criteria] which will make a **methodical investigation** and **presentation** of the **empirical material** possible. First and foremost, it is a *critical tool*. §986

## The facts of the types cannot be denied

**452** (1923, p. 628)
To **deny** the existence of types is **of little use** in face of the fact of their existence. §857

**453** (1923, p. 622)
It would certainly be **difficult** to adduce evidence **against** the existence of **psychological types**. §849

**454** (1923, p. 622)
I have no doubt at all that my opponents will be at some pains to eliminate the question of types from the scientific agenda. The **type problem** must be a **very unwelcome obstacle** for **every theory of complex psychic processes** that makes any **pretence** to **general validity**. §849

**455** (1923, p. 622)

**Every theory of complex psychic processes presupposes** uniform human psychology, following the analogy of **every natural science theory**, which also presupposes one and the same fundamental nature. §849

**456** (1921, p. 701 & 1923, p. 626)

Every living thing in the soul shimmers with many colours. For everyone who thinks there exists but one true explanation of a psychic process, this vitality of psychic contents is **a matter for despair**, especially if he should be a lover of simple and uncomplicated truths. §854

# BIBLIOGRAPHY

Jung, C.G. (1916) "A Contribution to the Study of Psychological Types," in *Collected Papers on Analytical Psychology*, ed. by Constance E. Long. London: Baillière, Tindall and Cox, 287-298.

Jung, C.G. (1921) *Psychologische Typen*. Zürich: Rascher.

Jung, C.G. (1923) *Psychological Types*, trans. H.G. Baynes. London: Routledge & Kegan Paul.

Jung, C.G. (1928) "Psychological Types," in *Contributions to Analytical Psychology*, trans. H.G. and Cary F. Baynes. London: Kegan Paul, Trench, Trubner, 295-312.

Jung, C.G.(1933) "A Psychological Theory of Types,"in *Modern Man in Search of A Soul,* trans. W.S. Dell and Cary F. Baynes. London: Routledge & Kegan Paul, 85-108.

Jung, C.G. "Psychologische Typologie", *Süddeutsche Monatshefte,* XXXIII: 5, (Feb. 1936), 264-72.

Jung, C.G. (1971) *The Collected Works of C.G. Jung,* Vol. 6, *Psychological Types*, eds. Herbert Read, Michael Fordham, Gerhard Adler, and William McGuire, rev. trans. of the H.G.Baynes translation by R.F.C. Hull. London: Routledge & Kegan Paul.

Jung, C.G. (1978) *C.G.Jung Gesammelte Werke,* Band 6, *Psychologische Typen,* eds. Marianne Niehus-Jung, Lena Hurwicht-Eisner, and Franz Riklin. Zürich: Walter-Verlag, 4th unchanged ed.

# ACKNOWLEDGEMENT

We would like to acknowledge the invaluable contributions made by our co-director, Sumi Gous, in shaping this publication since its inception. Throughout the process her critical questions kept us all on our toes and her inputs enriched the outcome. Her fine touch is tangible not only in the meticulous layout, but in particiular, she deserves special mention for the unique symbolic artwork created for the book cover.

ISBN 978-0-7961-7232-7

www.ingramcontent.com/pod-product-compliance
Lightning Source LLC
Chambersburg PA
CBHW051557030426
42334CB00034B/3466